What Kids
Need to
Succeed

Based on a nationwide survey of over
270,000 young people in 600 communities

What Kids
Need to
Succeed

Proven, Practical Ways
to Raise Good Kids

**Peter L. Benson, Ph.D., Judy Galbraith, M.A.,
and Pamela Espeland**

Free
Spirit®
PUBLISHING

Library of Congress Cataloging-in-Publication Data
Benson, Peter L.
      What kids need to succeed : proven, practical ways to raise good
   kids / Peter L. Benson, Judy Galbraith, and Pamela Espeland.
         p.   cm.
      "Based on a nationwide survey of over 270,000 young people in
   600 communities."
      Includes bibliographical references and index.
      ISBN 0-915793-78-4
      1. Child rearing–United States. 2. Parenting–United States.
   3. Self-esteem in children–United States. I. Galbraith, Judy.
   II. Espeland, Pamela. III. Title.
   HQ769.B5118 1994
   649'.1'0973–dc20   94-36533
                                                                  CIP

10 9 8 7 6 5 4 3 2

Printed in the United States of America
Cover and book design by MacLean & Tuminelly
Cover photo by Skjold Photographers
Index compiled by Theresa Wolner and Eileen Quam

What Kids Need to Succeed is based on *The Troubled Journey: A Portrait
of 6th–12th Grade Youth* by Peter L. Benson, Ph.D., published in 1993 by
Search Institute and sponsored by RespecTeen, a national program of
Lutheran Brotherhood, and on continuing research by Search Institute.
For more information about Search Institute, call toll-free:
1-800-888-7828
For more information about RespecTeen, call toll-free:
1-800-888-3820

Free Spirit Publishing Inc.
400 First Avenue North, Suite 616
Minneapolis, MN 55401-1730
(612) 338-2068
1-800-735-7323

Contents

What Do Kids Really Need?

Most adults today are deeply concerned about young people.

We're worried about our own kids, our neighbors' kids, the students in our classrooms, the youth in our congregations, and kids as a whole. We've seen the stories and the appalling facts about teen pregnancy, violence, school failure, substance abuse, sexually transmitted diseases, eating disorders, and suicide. We've watched the news and stared at images of alienated, angry kids who seem unreachable and doomed. We feel powerless to help because nothing—no program, initiative, strategy, or organization—seems to be working long enough, hard enough, or for enough kids.

It's depressing, frustrating, and frightening, but it doesn't have to be that way.

What if you knew that there are specific, practical things you can do to make a tremendous difference in young people's lives? What if you saw documented proof that these specific, practical things really work?

The title of this book, *What Kids Need to Succeed*, is not an exaggeration. It's a simple statement of what you'll find here: powerful ideas for positive change.

These ideas can assure a better future for the young people you know personally, for all young people in your community, and ultimately for everyone—if you're willing to try them.

What kids really need are adults who care.

This book began with a nationwide survey.

From September, 1989, through March, 1990, students in grades 6 through 12 were given a 152-item inventory called "Profiles of Student Life: Attitudes and Behaviors." The inventory was developed by Search Institute, a nonprofit organization based in Minneapolis, Minnesota, that specializes in research on children and youth. It was sponsored by RespecTeen, a national program of Lutheran Brotherhood in Minneapolis that helps communities develop strategies to promote youth welfare.

Over 46,000 students in 111 communities and 25 states took part in the initial survey. The results were published in 1990 by Lutheran Brotherhood and in 1993 by Search Institute as *The Troubled Journey: A Portrait of 6th–12th Grade Youth.*

Meanwhile, the survey continued and grew. To date, 273,000 young people in 600 communities and 33 states have taken the Search Institute inventory. They live in small towns, suburbs, and big cities; in traditional, single-parent, and adoptive families; in poverty, the middle class, and affluence. The facts reported here are based on the most recent findings available at this writing.

If you could survey 273,000 kids, you'd learn some amazing things.

When Search Institute started analyzing the information from the surveys, we discovered that the difference between troubled teens and those leading healthy, productive, positive lives was strongly affected by the presence of what we call **developmental assets.**

The usual definition of assets is "property or resources." We chose this term because the things we identified—building blocks for human development—act like assets in a young person's life. They increase in value over time. They provide a sense of security. They are resources upon which a child can draw again and again. And they're cumulative, meaning that *the more a young person has, the better.*

We identified 30 assets—good things that every young person needs in his or her life. The first 16 are **external assets,** or things in a young person's environment that support and nurture him or her, set boundaries, and involve the young person in structured time use with caring, principled adults. These assets are:

1. Family support
2. Parents as social resources
3. Parent communication
4. Other adult resources
5. Other adult communication
6. Parent involvement in school
7. Positive school climate
8. Parental standards
9. Parental discipline
10. Parental monitoring

11. Time at home

12. Positive peer influence

13. Music

14. Extracurricular activities

15. Community activities

16. Involvement with a faith community.

The next 14 are **internal assets**—attitudes, values, and competencies that belong in the head and heart of every child. These assets are:

17. Achievement motivation

18. Educational aspiration

19. School performance

20. Homework

21. Helping people

22. Global concern

23. Empathy

24. Sexual restraint

25. Assertiveness skills

26. Decision-making skills

27. Friendship-making skills

28. Planning skills

29. Self-esteem

30. Hope.

What Kids Need to Succeed describes the assets and gives you concrete, practical suggestions for building them in young people. As you can see, the assets aren't complicated. Most cost nothing in terms of money. Many are things you may already be doing. You won't find any radical, experimental, or theoretical ideas in this book. What you will find is a common-sense approach to raising good kids so they're free to grow into competent, contributing, responsible, compassionate adults.

In reality, there are probably dozens of other assets that are also important to helping teens succeed, but this list is a good beginning. If our kids could have many of these assets, we would all be a lot better off than we are today. As you start thinking seriously about asset-building, you'll likely find many other ways to provide positive support for the young people in your life.

Not every idea you'll read about here will work for everyone.

If you try an idea that doesn't work for a particular child or group, don't stop there. Keep reading! We've included *more than 500 ideas* for families, schools, communities, and congregations. There's bound to be one that gets results...then another, and another, and another.

This book does not attempt to describe everything you need to know or do before implementing an idea. For example, if we suggest that you recruit adult volunteers into a school, community organization, or congregation, you'll need to ensure that appropriate systems are in place to provide a safe, enriching environment for everyone, both kids *and* adults.

Despite the best efforts of concerned and involved adults, not every young person will end up with all 30 assets firmly in place. But it's important to remember that *the more assets a young person has, the better*. This is not wishful thinking. It's a fact that is clearly supported by the survey results.

How many of these assets do American kids have today? Although they should have at least 25, most have only 16—a start, but not enough. Here's a picture of what we found:

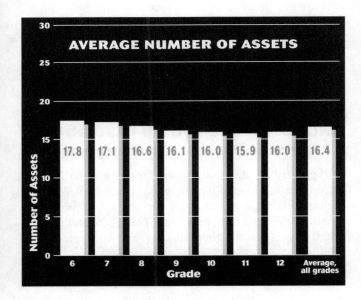

AVERAGE NUMBER OF ASSETS

Grade	Number of Assets
6	17.8
7	17.1
8	16.6
9	16.1
10	16.0
11	15.9
12	16.0
Average, all grades	16.4

How do we know that the total number of assets makes a difference? When we looked for specific at-risk behaviors—behaviors that are known to potentially limit psychological, physical, or economic well-being during adolescence or adulthood—we discovered how powerful the assets really are. *Young people who have more assets are much less likely to get involved in these problem behaviors.* See for yourself:

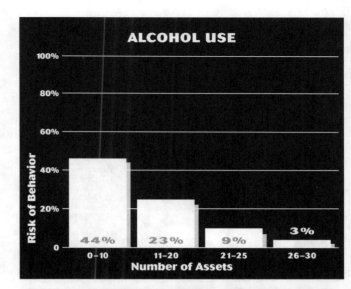

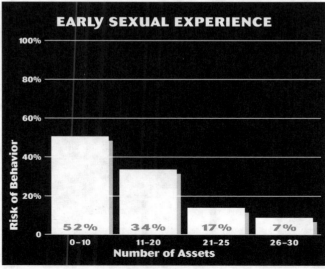

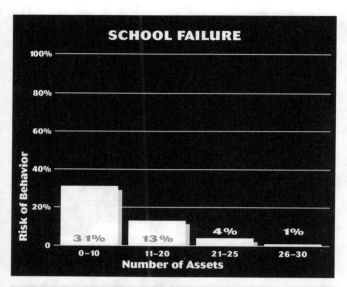

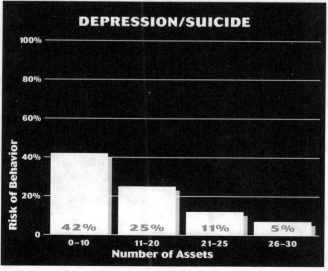

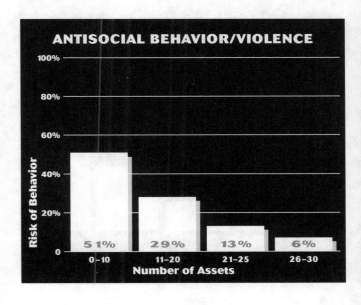

We also found that it works the other way—that young people who have more assets are much *more* likely to get involved in positive behaviors. Here is how the assets affect school success:

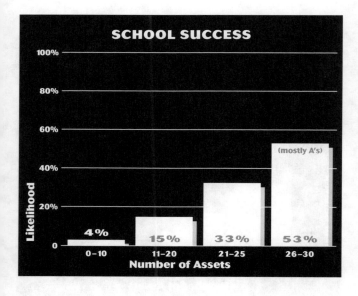

And here is how the assets influence what we call "caring behavior," which includes volunteering to help others and working with their communities to make a difference:

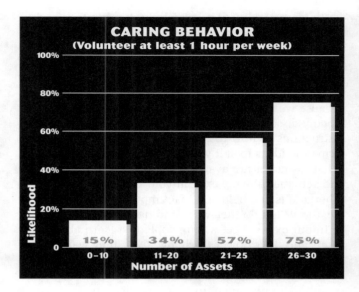

Whether you're a parent, a teacher, a community leader, a religious leader, or just an adult who wants to help kids, you can start building assets today.

This *positive* approach to youth development is not about crisis management, although young people who have these assets face fewer crises. It is not about stopping and preventing problems, although young people who have these assets face (and create) fewer problems. Instead, it's about investing wisely in our youth, increasing their exposure to positive, constructive activities, and instilling values and skills that will guide them from the inside.

Building assets is not a quick fix. It takes time and commitment from caring adults. It's worth it *because it works* and it makes all of our lives better.

This book presents literally hundreds of practical ideas for parents, schools, communities, and congregations to try. We have kept them brief and to the point, because we mean this to be an action handbook, not a lengthy dissertation. You won't find step-by-step instructions or how-tos. You'll need to decide how to shape the ideas to suit your particular circumstances. What resources are available to you? What programs and activities already exist in your community? What other adults can help you? Get input from young people, too. What do they want and need?

In our experience, when people first learn about the assets and their power to change lives, they want to get started right away. Use this book as a jumping-off point. Get together with your family, friends, and neighbors to plan ways to try these ideas in your community. Brainstorm your own ideas.

Throughout this book, you'll also find special sections called "Tips for Teens: Build Your Own Assets." Share these with the young people you know. You may want to start by telling them about the study and showing them the charts on pages 6–11. Most kids really want to stay out of trouble and succeed in life. When they understand how powerful the assets can be, they may decide to get involved in shaping their own future.

A few words about some of the words we use.

We use the words *parents* and *parent* throughout this book to indicate children's primary caregivers. Of course, not all kids live with two biological parents or even one biological parent. Rather than spell out "biological parent, step-parent, foster parent, adoptive parent, grandparent, guardian, or whatever" each time we refer to a primary caregiver, we've opted for simplicity and brevity. If you are an adult who is raising and guiding a teenager, then when we say "parent," we mean you.

We use the word *congregation* to indicate the people you worship with and *place of worship* to indicate where you go. We have chosen these more general terms over "church," "temple," "synagogue," "mosque," "meeting house," and others that refer more explicitly to specific faiths because we want to be sure to communicate the importance of asset-building in *all* faith communities and traditions.

This book has been written for a broad, general audience. As you share the information and discuss the assets with others, we hope you will use the words that feel most comfortable to you.

Please let us know how the ideas in this book work for you.

We welcome your suggestions for building assets in youth, and we would love to hear your success stories. You may write to us at this address:

Free Spirit Publishing Inc.
400 First Avenue North, Suite 616
Minneapolis, MN 55401-1730

It is our hope that building assets will become a national effort—that people in every community will work to create a better, more positive future for all children.

Let's get started.

Peter L. Benson, Ph.D.
Judy Galbraith, M.A.
Pamela Espeland

Add Up Your Assets: Checklists for Kids and Parents

How many assets does your child already have?

Most of the kids we surveyed have 16 assets out of the 30 we identified. If you're a parent, you're probably wondering how many assets your child already has. The checklists that follow can help you find out.

The checklist on pages 16–17 is for kids themselves; the one on pages 18–19 is for parents. Both are adaptations of the original Search Institute youth survey.

1. Start by making photocopies of each checklist. You may have more than one child, and you may want to return to the checklists later, after trying some of the suggestions in this book, so we recommend that you not write in the book itself.

2. Complete the checklists separately. Have each person total his or her responses.

3. Afterward, meet with your child to share and discuss your responses and perceptions. Does your child report more or fewer assets than you expected? Do you and your child have different ideas about the assets that are present in your child's life? You may be surprised by something your child says. If so, try saying, "I didn't know that! Tell me more...." As you'll see, the checklists provide a great opportunity for conversation and discovery.

Parents and kids who have talked about the checklists have found this to be an enriching experience in and of itself. It's also an asset-builder. When you take the time to talk seriously about the checklists, you're strengthening Asset #3: Parent Communication.

On each checklist, the numbers of the statements correspond to the numbers assigned to the assets. You may want to identify the assets that seem to be missing from your child's life, then turn immediately to the pages in this book that describe ways to build those assets.

A Checklist for Kids

Check each statement that is true for you.

❏   1.   I feel loved and supported in my family.

❏   2.   My parents are approachable when I have something serious to talk about.

❏   3.   I regularly have in-depth conversations with my parents.

❏   4.   In addition to my parents, I have three or more adults in my life I can go to for help.

❏   5.   I have frequent serious conversations with an adult who is not my parent.

❏   6.   My parents talk with me about school, sometimes help me with my schoolwork, and attend school events.

❏   7.   The atmosphere at my school is caring and encouraging.

❏   8.   My parents clearly express their standards for my behavior.

❏   9.   My parents set rules for me and enforce the consequences when I break the rules.

❏   10.   When I go out, my parents check on where I'm going, who I'll be with, and how long I'll be gone.

❏   11.   The number of nights I can spend out of the house for fun and recreation is limited.

❏   12.   My friends are a good influence on me. They are doing well at school and staying away from risky behaviors such as alcohol and other drug use.

❑ 13. I'm involved in band, orchestra, or choir or take lessons on a musical instrument. I practice one or more hours a week.

❑ 14. I participate in school sports activities or other organizations one or more hours a week.

❑ 15. I participate in non-school sports or other organizations one or more hours a week.

❑ 16. I attend a religious program or service at least once a month.

❑ 17. I try to do my best at school.

❑ 18. I hope to continue my education beyond high school.

❑ 19. My grades are above average.

❑ 20. I do six or more hours of homework a week.

❑ 21. I'm interested in helping others and trying to improve their lives.

❑ 22. I'm concerned about global issues such as world hunger.

❑ 23. I care about other people's feelings.

❑ 24. My values prohibit me from having sex as a teenager.

❑ 25. I can stick up for my beliefs.

❑ 26. I'm good at making decisions.

❑ 27. I'm good at making friends.

❑ 28. I'm good at planning ahead.

❑ 29. I feel good about myself.

❑ 30. I envision a happy future for myself.

A Checklist for Parents

Check each statement that is true for you or your child.

❑   1. I provide a warm, caring environment for my child at home.

❑   2. I'm approachable when my child has something serious to talk about.

❑   3. I frequently take time to talk seriously with my child.

❑   4. In addition to being able to come to me, my child has three or more adults he or she can go to for help.

❑   5. My child has frequent serious conversations with an adult who is not his or her parent.

❑   6. I talk with my child about school, sometimes help my child with schoolwork, and attend school events.

❑   7. The atmosphere at my child's school is caring and encouraging.

❑   8. I clearly express my standards for my child's behavior.

❑   9. I set rules for my child and enforce the consequences when rules are broken.

❑   10. When my child goes out, I check on where he or she is going, who with, and for how long.

❑   11. I limit the number of nights my child can spend out of the home for fun and recreation.

❑   12. My child's friends are a good influence. They do well at school and avoid risky behaviors such as alcohol and other drug use.

❑ 13. My child is involved in band, orchestra, or choir or takes lessons on a musical instrument. He or she practices one or more hours a week.

❑ 14. My child participates in school sports activities or other organizations one or more hours a week.

❑ 15. My child participates in non-school sports or other organizations one or more hours a week.

❑ 16. My child attends a religious program or service at least once a month.

❑ 17. My child tries to do his or her best at school.

❑ 18. My child hopes to continue his or her education beyond high school.

❑ 19. My child's grades are above average.

❑ 20. My child does six or more hours of homework a week.

❑ 21. My child is interested in helping others and trying to improve their lives.

❑ 22. My child shows concern for global issues such as world hunger.

❑ 23. My child cares about other people's feelings.

❑ 24. My child has values that prohibit him or her from having sex as a teenager.

❑ 25. My child can stick up for his or her beliefs.

❑ 26. My child is good at making decisions.

❑ 27. My child is good at making friends.

❑ 28. My child is good at planning ahead.

❑ 29. My child feels good about himself or herself.

❑ 30. My child envisions a happy future for himself or herself.

Building External Assets

Support

Young people need caring, principled adults in their lives who support them, encourage them, and guide them. They need places to be—home, school, neighborhood, congregation, work—that are accepting, affirming, and safe. Following are ideas to try at home, at school, in the community, and in the congregation.

ASSET #1:

Family Support

Kids feel loved and supported in their family.

> **57%** *of the youth we surveyed have this asset in their lives.*

At Home

▶ Give more hugs and verbal reinforcement. Don't assume that your kids know how much you love them–tell them.

▶ Let your love for your children show in the way you look at them, the words you say, your tone of voice, and your body language.

▶ It's not true that all kids want their parents to stop hugging them once they become teenagers. Ask your children to tell you what feels comfortable for them, and respect their boundaries.

▶ Set aside at least one evening per week for family activities. Brainstorm as a family things you might like to do, then agree on which ones to try. Be open to ideas from all family members, and be willing to share your children's interests.

▶ Spend time with each of your children individually. Try to make this a daily event–ten minutes after school, a half-hour before bedtime, an hour on Saturday morning. Let them know that your time together is important to you, too.

▶ Talk with your kids about what would make your home more comfortable and inviting for them and their friends. Take steps to address any concerns.

At School

▶ Educate parents on how to be supportive of their children. Check with your school counselor or social worker for suggestions.

▶ Regularly call or write parents to give positive messages about their child's attitude or progress, or to report on something the child did that deserves praise and recognition. Do this as often as you can— once every month, three or four times during the school year, or whatever is possible for you.

In the Community

▶ Offer workshops for parents on positive parenting skills. Invite experts to speak on ways for parents to show love and support to their children. Allow time for parents to share their ideas and experiences.

▶ Provide and publicize family crisis hotlines. These give family members a chance to "cool off" during a conflict. Train hotline counselors to suggest appropriate ways to respond to conflict, and to refer parents to other resources.

In the Congregation

▶ Sponsor family nights as a regular part of your youth programming.

▶ Make sure that your youth program isn't overplanned. Leave time for families to spend together.

ASSET #2:

Parents as Social Resources

**Kids turn to parents for advice and support.
Parents are approachable and available when
kids have something serious to talk about.**

46% *of the youth we surveyed
have this asset in their lives.*

At Home

▶ Ask your kids *every day* about what they are doing
and thinking about. Start with simple questions like
"What did you do in school today?" "Did you get a
chance to talk with your teacher about the science
fair project?" "What do think of the news about...?"
Form the habit of daily conversation.

▶ Make it clear to your children that you value their
opinions, knowledge, feelings, and experiences.
Really *listen* to what they say.

▶ Give your kids space when they need it, but let them
know you're always available—and then *be* available.
What if you're in the middle of something? Try saying, "I can't talk right this minute. Can you wait ten
minutes or so?" Then be ready in ten minutes to
give your child your full attention.

▶ Remember that some kids have a hard time sitting still. They may need to wiggle and move around. Don't insist that they "settle down" before you're willing to listen and talk.

▶ Be willing to talk in a place that's comfortable for the child, whether it's your child's room, the middle of the kitchen floor, a tree house, or a fast-food restaurant. It's okay if there's music playing in the background, but turn off the television.

At School

▶ Include conversations with parents as part of home-work assignments. For example, if you're teaching about the 1960s, you might assign parent inter-views– "Where were you in 1969, and what were you doing? How did you feel about the war in Viet Nam?"

▶ Provide parents with information about how to respond to tough issues. Check with your school counselor or social worker about handouts and brochures on alcohol and other drugs, AIDS, teen pregnancy, sexual behavior, and other difficult top-ics. Many parents want to talk with their kids about these subjects, but they don't know where to start or what to say.

In the Community

▶ Teach parents how to respond appropriately when difficult issues arise. Offer workshops and commu-nity meetings on topics of concern to your community. Invite experts to speak on ways to talk with and listen to kids of all ages.

▶ Sponsor activities and events that bring young people and parents together. Build in time for conversation.

In the Congregation

▶ Plan parent-teen events that encourage conversation—dinners, retreats, discussion groups.

▶ Educate parents about how to support youth. Include articles and suggestions in mailings to member households. Let parents know that there is someone on staff who is available to answer questions, offer advice, and just listen. Parents need social resources, too.

ASSET #3:

Parent Communication

**Kids have frequent, in-depth conversations
with parents on a variety of topics.
Parents take the time to talk seriously
with their children.**

> **48%** *of the youth we surveyed
> have this asset in their lives.*

At Home

▶ Be available whenever and wherever your kids want
to talk. If you really can't talk right then and there,
arrange a time and place when you can talk...soon.

▶ Regularly ask your kids about what they think and
believe. Use questions, not challenges. Accept and
respect the fact that you won't agree on everything.

▶ Never label a child's beliefs as "silly," "stupid,"
"childish," or "wrong." Remarks like "You may
believe this now, but when you're older..." are guar-
anteed conversation stoppers.

▶ Have special family dinners in which the whole conversation focuses on one topic. Brainstorm as a
family things you might talk about, then rotate
whose turn it is to pick the topic.

▶ Spend one-on-one time with each of your children—
a whole day, if possible. Take a long drive, visit the
zoo, go shopping, or go on a picnic. You'll probably
end up talking about all sorts of things.

▶ Don't assume that your children aren't in touch with what's happening in the world. Many kids are very aware of and deeply disturbed by news reports of famine, violence, atrocities, and terrorism, often accompanied by frightening images and grisly facts. They need to talk with caring, supportive adults about what they have seen and heard.

▶ The fewer topics you declare "off limits," the more your kids will talk to you. If you don't know the answer to a question, help your kids to find it. Visit the library together, ask an expert, do some research. Exception: It's perfectly reasonable to set boundaries about certain questions pertaining to your personal life.

At School

▶ Interact with students so they learn to interact with others. Make time in the classroom to talk about serious issues and troublesome questions. If you don't know the answer to a question, offer to find the answer, ask for volunteers to research the answer, or invite an expert in to talk to the class.

▶ Role-play family conversations in the classroom so kids can learn to express their feelings. Help them develop a feelings vocabulary. Use posters, films, and literature to explore feelings and ways to express them.

In the Community

▶ Sponsor discussion nights for parents and teens. Publicize the topics in advance.

▶ Offer study guides for family discussions around current issues. Invite parents and kids to suggest topics, then ask experts to prepare questions, background information, and lists of resources.

In the Congregation

▶ Provide families with conversation-starter questions in the worship bulletin. Sponsor discussion groups around issues and questions.

▶ Teach communication skills to young people and adults. There may be a communications expert in your congregation who can donate time and expertise.

ASSET #4:
Other Adult Resources

**Kids have other adults besides their parents
they can turn to for advice and support.
Ideally, three or more adults play this
role in their lives.**

49% *of the youth we surveyed
have this asset in their lives.*

At Home

▶ Give your children opportunities to spend time with
  other adults. Is there a trusted neighbor, a favorite
  teacher, an adult relative, or a youth group leader
  your kids feel comfortable with and like? These
  adults can all be positive influences in their lives.

▶ Have family vacations with other families so your
  kids have opportunities to spend time with other
  adults.

▶ Many schools, youth organizations, and congregations have people on staff–guidance counselors,
  psychologists, and others–who are specially trained
  to work with young people. Encourage your children
  to meet these individuals, and explain that it's okay
  with you if they want to talk to them.

▶ Take an active role in your neighborhood and community. Through you, your children may meet other
  adults they will eventually get to know.

▶ When you invite friends over for social occasions, include their children and your children in your plans. Sharing a dinner, playing board games, and playing volleyball are all opportunities for interaction.

At School

▶ Take time to ask students at least one personal question at every student conference or one-on-one meeting. This shows that you're interested in them as individuals. You might ask something as simple as, "How do you feel about the school year so far?"

▶ Be the faculty sponsor for a student club. You'll get to know a group of kids who share a common interest, and you'll relate to them differently outside the classroom.

▶ Work with people in your community to arrange mentoring, internship, and service-learning opportunities for students.

In the Community

▶ Offer mentoring programs that match kids with caring adults. Offer to be a mentor.

▶ Sponsor career days for young people to spend time with adults in interesting professions.

▶ Pair kids with adult volunteers for community service projects.

In the Congregation

▶ Train adult volunteers to talk with kids who have concerns. Publicize the fact that these volunteers are available and accessible.

▶ Sponsor a congregational mentoring program.

ASSET #5:

Other Adult Communication

Kids have frequent, in-depth conversations with adults who are not their parents.

41% *of the youth we surveyed have this asset in their lives.*

At Home

▶ Encourage your children to call an adult friend they respect when they need advice.

▶ Include your kids in conversations you have in your home with other adults.

▶ If your child has a special interest or passion—computers, basketball, music, video games, collecting trading cards, bicycling, or whatever it might be—arrange for him or her to meet an adult friend of yours who shares that passion.

▶ Encourage your children to join adult-sponsored groups, troops, or teams.

At School

▶ Occasionally eat lunch in the cafeteria with the students.

▶ Don't consider it wasted time when teachers spend time talking with students.

▶ Be available to talk with students once a week (or more often) after school. Have an open-door policy; anyone who wants to stop by is welcome.

▶ Let parents know that there are people on staff who are willing and available to talk with kids.

In the Community

▶ Teach coaches and other volunteers how to communicate well with teens.

▶ Have adults work and play alongside youth.

▶ Encourage coaches and other adult leaders to make a special effort to get to know the young people on their teams and in their groups.

In the Congregation

▶ Teach volunteers about how to communicate with youth.

▶ Plan intergenerational programs and events in which kids and adults get to know one another.

ASSET #6:

Parent Involvement in School

Parents are involved in helping young people succeed in school. They talk with their kids about school, sometimes assist with schoolwork, and attend school events.

> **26%** *of the youth we surveyed have this asset in their lives.*

At Home

▶ Make it a point to talk with all of your child's teachers at least once during the school year.

▶ Regularly ask your kids what they are learning in school. Offer to help with homework in appropriate ways. For example, it's okay to help a child plan a special paper and to be available for advice, suggestions, or rides to the library. It's *not* okay to write the paper.

▶ When you receive a school calendar, enter important dates and events onto your family calendar. Make attending school events a priority within your family.

▶ Join the parent-teacher organization at your child's school.

▶ Volunteer to do what you can to help out at your child's school. Be a room parent, chaperone school functions, serve on committees.

▶ If you are concerned about circumstances or events at your child's school, talk to teachers and administrators. If you feel unheard, talk to other parents about constructive ways to address those concerns.

At School

▶ Personally contact each student's family at least once during the school year.

▶ Form a parent advisory committee to give input into school policy decisions.

▶ Send notes home to parents frequently about what the students are working on and learning in class.

▶ If you publish a class newsletter, print additional copies for your students to bring home to their parents.

In the Community

▶ Coordinate activities with the school(s) so parents don't have to choose between school events and community events.

▶ On days when schools have open houses and parent-teacher conferences, provide activities for children so parents are free to participate.

In the Congregation

▶ Don't schedule activities for youth that conflict with important school activities.

▶ Encourage parents to show an interest in their children's school experience and to take any concerns they have to the school.

▶ Offer workshops for parents on how to get involved and stay involved in their children's school.

ASSET #7:
Positive School Climate

School provides a caring, encouraging, and safe environment for kids.

31% *of the youth we surveyed have this asset in their lives.*

At Home

▶ Ask your children to tell you about any school-related fears or concerns they might have. Are they worried about bullies? Are there fights on the playground? Do the hallways feel safe? The bathrooms? The lunchroom?

▶ Report any concerns you have about your children feeling uncomfortable or unsafe in school. Call or write to the principal directly. When you write, request a response.

▶ Ask to see your school's policy book and student handbook. These publications will tell you about school safety policies already in place, the expectations the school has for student behavior, and the consequences for violating school rules and guidelines. Read them carefully and contact the principal about any questions you have. Go over the student handbook with your child and make sure that he or she understands it.

▶ Join or start a parent safety committee at your child's school. Tour the school and identify safety violations or concerns. Work with the school administration to address these issues.

▶ Volunteer in the school to tutor and support students. The more time you spend at your child's school, the more you'll know about what really goes on there.

At School

▶ Create an environment where everyone—students, staff, administrators, parents—feels cared for, supported, included, and important. Personalize your school as much as possible.

▶ Nurture a sense of school ownership in students by involving them in decision-making about issues that matter to them. For example, if there's a problem in the hallways, form a student committee to research, report on, and help to fix the problem. Invite student representatives to attend meetings about school concerns.

▶ Start a "school problem box" so students can report problems, articulate concerns, and suggest solutions.

In the Community

▶ Encourage young people to talk about school and their school experiences. Work to break down the barriers between school and the "real world."

▶ The "neighborhood school" may be a thing of the past, but you can still support the schools in your community. Send representatives to school fairs,

concerts, and other functions. Ask for volunteers to
tutor in the schools or help out in other ways.

▶ When you sponsor activities for young people, break
down school cliques by mixing teens into random
groups. Help them get to know other kids in their
school and other schools.

In the Congregation

▶ When the youth group looks for service projects,
don't forget nearby schools. The young people might
volunteer to paint, work on the grounds, make simple repairs, or help out in other ways.

▶ Encourage congregation members to volunteer in
the schools. Parents can volunteer in their own children's schools; adults who don't have children, or
whose children are grown, can volunteer in nearby
schools.

Tips for Teens: Build Your Own Assets

Asset #1: Family Support

GOAL: A family that is loving and supportive, and a home that is a comfortable place to be.

If you want a warm, caring, comfortable, and fun environment at home, do your part to make it that way. Replace put-downs with affirmations, teasing with supporting, thinking "me" with thinking "we." Show some affection, show some interest, and listen when other people want to talk. Treat the people in your family the way you want them to treat you. These ideas may sound simple, but they're very powerful tools for positive change.

Asset #2: Parents as Social Resources

GOAL: Parents you can turn to for advice and support.

Whenever you ask your parents for advice or support, does it turn into a lecture? This is a common problem. It helps to understand that for most parents, giving advice is an almost irresistible urge. You might try explaining that sometimes all you really need them to do is listen while you sort things out. Or suggest a compromise: You talk, they just listen, and ten minutes later (or an hour, or a day) you listen to what they have to say.

Another idea to try: Find things your parents are really good at, then focus on those. For example, if your mom is a math whiz, turn to her when you get stuck on your homework or you're worried about the math final. If your dad likes to write, ask for his advice on the article you're writing for your school newspaper. You may learn something new, and your parents will be delighted by the experience.

Asset #3: Parent Communication

GOAL: Parents you can talk to about serious topics.

If you feel that you can't talk to your parents about the serious issues in your life, maybe it's because they still treat you like a child. It's hard for parents to accept that their children are growing up and forming their own beliefs and opinions. If there's another adult in your life you can talk to—someone who values your opinions and treats you with respect—try to arrange a meeting between you, your parents, and the other adult. Maybe your parents will see you through that person's eyes.

It's normal for kids and parents to disagree about serious issues. Try to stay calm, and keep your voice down. Meanwhile, make an effort to see your parents' point of view. You'll be setting a good example for them to follow.

Asset #4: Other Adult Resources

GOAL: Adults besides your parents you can turn to for advice and support.

If you don't have other adults to talk to, start looking in the places you normally go—your school, place of worship, scout troop, neighborhood park, or community center. You'll probably find adults who enjoy spending time with young people. Or see if there is a teen clinic in your area. Most (if not all) offer counseling, not just medical advice.

Asset #5: Other Adult Communication

GOAL: Adults besides your parents you can talk to about serious topics.

Join an adult-sponsored group, troop, or team. Meet your neighbors. Talk to your school counselor or the youth leader at your place of worship. Have a heart-to-heart with a favorite aunt or uncle. Get to know your friends' parents. You *will* find adults you can talk to, if you're willing to reach out and make the effort.

Asset #6: Parent Involvement in School

GOAL: Parents who are personally involved in helping you to succeed in school.

Talk to your parents about school. Tell them about your day, your successes, your frustrations. Share funny stories with them. Ask them to help you with a school project or a sticky homework problem. Let them know that you really *want* them to be involved.

If your teachers send notes, schedules, and announcements home with you, be sure to give them to your parents. Offer to write important school events on the family calendar. Remind them of special events a few days in advance.

Asset #7: Positive School Climate

GOAL: A school that's safe, encouraging, and caring.

Tell your parents about any fears or concerns you have about school. Describe any events that made you feel worried or afraid. Also tell about the things you enjoy most about school. Don't just focus on the negatives.

Encourage your parents to volunteer in the school, if at all possible. Often parents don't know what goes on in school until they spend time there themselves.

Get involved in school activities—sports teams, student government, service groups, the school paper. You'll feel more positive about school because you're more involved.

Do your part to make your school safer and more caring. Start or join a student group, brainstorm ideas, and take them to the administration. Volunteer to help put your ideas into action.

Boundaries

Young people need the adults in their lives to set standards and rules, enforce reasonable consequences, and care about their whereabouts. Following are ideas to try at home, at school, in the community, and in the congregation.

ASSET #8:

Parental Standards

Parents have standards for appropriate conduct. They clearly express their standards to their kids.

76% *of the youth we surveyed have this asset in their lives.*

At Home

▶ Clarify your standards to yourself and your spouse. Make sure that you agree on your expectations for your children's behavior. Kids need parents to stand together on important issues—to be consistent and not contradict each other.

▶ Regularly review your standards for your children's conduct. Are they reasonable and fair? Are they respectful of your children's needs? Read current parenting books and seek expert advice if you have questions or need help. Be willing to learn and change.

▶ Talk to your children about your standards and why they are important to you and your family. Articulate them clearly using words that your children can understand. Be ready to give reasons for your standards; your children will probably ask, and "because I said so" is not an answer that leads to understanding and acceptance.

- ▶ Invite your kids to articulate their standards with you. Help them to clarify their own understanding. Often you'll find that your standards and theirs are more similar than different.
- ▶ Regularly renegotiate family rules with teenagers so they are appropriate for their age and maturity level.
- ▶ When you're not sure how to respond to a particular situation, talk with other parents. Teachers can also be good sources of information and advice, as can school counselors, social workers, or psychologists, community leaders, and religious leaders.

At School

- ▶ Respect and reinforce family values and rules as much as possible.
- ▶ Talk with parents about their standards for their children's conduct, and share with them your standards for student conduct. Find common ground and reinforce each others' efforts.
- ▶ Set clear expectations for students in the school. Make rules known to parents and to youth. If you publish a student handbook that outlines rules and expectations, make copies available to parents.

In the Community

- ▶ Educate parents about appropriate limits for teens. Invite experts to speak on ways for parents to define and enforce limits. Allow time for parents to ask questions, share stories, and make suggestions.

▶ Offer parent support groups so parents can learn from each other about establishing and maintaining appropriate standards for their children's conduct.

In the Congregation

▶ Set and enforce clear expectations for the behavior of the youth in your congregation.

▶ Educate parents about how to set appropriate limits and boundaries. Include ideas in worship bulletins and mailings to member households.

▶ Give parents opportunities to talk together about appropriate standards for their children.

▶ Educate young people about how to set limits and boundaries for themselves. This would be an excellent topic for a youth retreat.

ASSET #9:
Parental Discipline

Parents set rules for kids with fair and reasonable consequences. They enforce the consequences when rules are broken.

58% *of the youth we surveyed have this asset in their lives.*

At Home

▶ Work with your spouse to determine the rules and consequences for your children. Make sure that you agree on important issues. Each parent should have the authority to set rules and carry out the consequences for breaking the rules.

▶ Invite your children to take part in conversations about rules and consequences. When kids are treated respectfully and taken seriously, they come up with good ideas. Try letting your kids determine their own consequences for breaking certain rules.

▶ Be consistent in communicating and enforcing rules. On the other hand, be willing to review and renegotiate rules and consequences as your children get older and circumstances change. It's perfectly reasonable for some rules to vary according to each child's age and maturity level.

▶ Focus discipline as a way to teach, not as a form of punishment. Remember that the best discipline grows out of mutual respect and strong relationships, not out of the authoritarian use of power.

▶ Never let discipline become an excuse for venting anger with violence. If you are at all concerned about physical or emotional abuse, or if you feel that things sometimes get out of hand, seek help. Call a local crisis hotline and ask for information on support groups for parents.

▶ If your children keep breaking rules, explore the reasons rather than just clamping down. You may discover that their acting out is a result of unmet needs, emotional or psychological issues, or medical concerns.

At School

▶ Have clearly established rules and consequences for student behavior at school. Enforce consequences consistently and fairly.

▶ When a child has a behavior problem, inform the parents. Clearly explain the problem and the consequences. Ask for the parents' support. Get their insights into issues that may be contributing to the problem. For example, a child might be acting out because of a death in the family, a divorce, or another important change in the family.

▶ Include parents in meetings with students regarding problem behaviors and broken rules.

In the Community

▶ As you set standards for young people's participation in community activities, invite parents to contribute their ideas and suggestions.

▶ Create tip sheets for parents on fair and effective discipline strategies.

▶ Offer workshops for parents on ways to address problem behaviors, how to set fair rules, and how to enforce consequences. Invite experts to speak and field questions.

▶ Work with others in the community to begin identifying and naming appropriate community norms and standards. Include young people in the process.

▶ Work with local businesses, neighborhood organizations, and law enforcement agencies to identify places where kids get into trouble. Start a series of community meetings to identify and implement solutions.

In the Congregation

▶ Respect and reinforce parents' rules and consequences—unless they are abusive.

▶ Educate parents in appropriate strategies for setting rules and enforcing consequences. Include ideas in worship bulletins and mailings to member households. Hold workshops for parents.

ASSET #10:

Parental Monitoring

Parents monitor their children's whereabouts. When kids go out, parents check on where they are going, who they will be with, what they will be doing, and how long they will be gone.

76% *of the youth we surveyed have this asset in their lives.*

At Home

▶ Have a family calendar with lots of writing space for *everyone* to note appointments, social events, meetings, and special occasions. This helps family members keep track of one another and facilitates communication.

▶ When you go out, let your children know where you're going and approximately how long you'll be gone. Leave a telephone number so they can contact you in the event of an emergency. This isn't "kid monitoring," it's good role modeling of considerate behavior.

▶ When your children must be home alone, call them and ask them about what they are doing. Unsupervised children are less likely to get into trouble if their parents stay in touch with them.

▶ Whenever your kids announce plans to attend parties or other activities, ask *who* they will be with, *what* they will be doing, *where* they will be, and *when* they will depart and return. Make this a habit and a rule.

▶ Make sure that parents are always present for parties and get-togethers at other kids' homes. If you're not sure, call ahead to find out. Accompany your child to the home and take this opportunity to introduce yourself to the parents.

▶ Find out who your children's friends are, then invite their parents to form a "parent network" with you. Agree to chaperone your children's parties. Agree that children will not be allowed to hold or attend parties without adult supervision.

▶ Make your home an inviting place for your kids and their friends. When they're home, you know where they are!

At School

▶ Inform parents in advance about any special trips or extended programs. Invite parents to chaperone.

▶ Tell parents when a student skips classes or leaves school at inappropriate times.

▶ Provide adequate adult supervision in the lunchroom, in the hallways, on the playground, and other places where students gather.

In the Community

▶ Use parent consent forms for trips and special activities.

▶ Create an agreement form for kids and parents on which they both agree to keep the other informed about their whereabouts. Publicize the form, introduce it at a community meeting, and have copies available.

▶ When you see young people in inappropriate places, take responsibility to ask them whether their parents know where they are.

In the Congregation

▶ Keep parents well-informed about youth activities. Include announcements of upcoming activities and brief reports on recent activities in worship bulletins and mailings.

▶ Provide adequate adult supervision for all youth group events.

ASSET #11:
Time at Home

Kids spend time at home at least four nights a week. Parents limit the number of nights children can spend out of the home for fun or recreation.

68% *of the youth we surveyed have this asset in their lives.*

At Home

▶ Set limits on how often kids can go out with their friends during the school week. Have a family meeting to determine what seems reasonable and fair, starting with the basic guideline of four nights at home.

▶ If your teenager has a part-time job, limit it to 15 hours a week or less during the school year. Studies have shown that teenagers who work more than 15 hours a week have more problems than those who work fewer hours.

▶ Be firm about the four nights at home, but not inflexible. Kids should have the opportunity to participate in activities that are important to them, such as the school play or a sports tournament, even if it means being away from home more often than usual for a period of time.

▶ Allow your children to invite friends over on their "at home" nights—not all of the time, but some of the time. (Maybe the science study group could meet at your house.)

▶ Plan to be home with your children. Sit down to dinner together. Be available to help with homework or just talk.

▶ Spend time together doing things you enjoy as a family. Play favorite games, have a family video night, read, take walks or bike rides.

▶ Make your home a pleasant place for all family members—somewhere your kids want to be. If you feel that family members argue too much or have trouble communicating, seek outside help. Family counselors are expert in helping families to get along better.

At School

▶ Limit the number of nights in one week that students can be involved in school activities. Train adult leaders in helping kids to set priorities.

▶ Encourage coaches, club sponsors, and others not to overschedule students.

▶ Spread special school events over the whole school year instead of grouping them around holidays or other occasions.

In the Community

▶ Limit the number of nights youth are expected to participate in activities.

▶ Create community calendars that include all different kinds of youth activities—in schools, congregations, community organizations, etc. Distribute them widely (perhaps through local access cable or a community newspaper) so families can plan and set priorities together.

▶ Sponsor workshops for parents on communicating with kids. Offer suggestions for activities and projects families can do together.

▶ Limit the number of nights adults are expected to participate in activities so they can spend more time at home with their children.

In the Congregation

▶ Encourage families to schedule regular "family nights." Offer suggestions for activities and projects to do as a family. Include ideas in worship bulletins and mailings to member households.

▶ Limit the number of evenings youth are expected to participate in activities related to your youth program.

ASSET #12:
Positive Peer Influence

Children's best friends model responsible behavior. They are a good influence. They do well at school and stay away from risky behaviors such as alcohol and other drug use.

31% *of the youth we surveyed have this asset in their lives.*

At Home

▶ Invite your children's friends to spend time in your home. Make them feel welcome and try to get to know them. Include them in some of your family activities.

▶ Talk with your kids about their friends. Ask probing questions. Are they good students? What are their interests? Do they get along well with their parents? Try to find out what your children like about their friends.

▶ Affirm positive friendships without going overboard. You might say something like, "Jeff seems like a nice kid. He's funny and easy to be around. I'm glad you invite him over."

▶ Resist the urge to criticize friendships that seem negative. Many kids get defensive about friends their parents don't like. This makes them even more determined to maintain the friendships.

▶ Get to know the parents of your children's friends. Have your kids introduce you at school open houses, community meetings, or activities at your place of worship.

At School

▶ Train students to be peer counselors or peer helpers. Choose kids who can become good role models and who are liked by their peers.

▶ Provide cooperative learning opportunities for students. Let students work together in groups. Make sure that all children benefit from the cooperative learning experience. For example, the bright students shouldn't spend all or most of their time tutoring other students.

▶ Use class time to teach about friendship. Challenge kids to think about their own friendships. Are they helpful or hurtful? How can they tell? Help children develop the skills they need to make and keep good friends.

In the Community

▶ Provide opportunities for young people to model healthy behavior for one another. Helping others through community service is one way to set a great example.

▶ Affirm and honor the healthy choices that youth make. Invite kids to create posters against drug and alcohol use and/or violence, then sign them and display them in the community. Publish the names of honor students in local newspapers. Encourage the media to do feature stories on young people who are making a difference in the community.

▶ Sponsor an awards night for young people in the community who serve as good role models. Adults and kids could nominate deserving youth by secret ballot.

In the Congregation

▶ Start a peer ministry program. Train young people to be good listeners and to offer appropriate advice and suggestions. Train them to know when and how to seek help from adults.

▶ Invite young people to think about ways to positively influence their friends in school and in the community. This would be an excellent topic for a weekend youth retreat.

▶ Affirm and honor the young role models in your congregation.

▶ Make friendship a regular topic of discussion within your youth program. Ask kids about their friends. Ask them to think about how their friendships fit with their values.

▶ Sponsor events for youth that include their friends from outside the congregation.

Tips for Teens:
Build Your Own Assets

Asset #8: Parental Standards

GOAL: Parents who have standards for your behavior and clearly express them to you.

You need to know what your parents expect of you—their standards for your behavior. If you don't know, ask. Take this opportunity to tell your parents what's important to you—what you believe in, and the decisions you have made for yourself. They will be glad to know, for example, that you have made a personal pledge not to use alcohol and other drugs. As your parents watch you make good decisions, they will become more comfortable with your standards. Meanwhile, you may discover that your standards and your parents' standards are more similar than you think.

Asset #9: Parental Discipline

GOAL: Parents who set rules with fair and reasonable consequences, then enforce the consequences when you break the rules.

What are the rules around your house? If you don't know, find out. Talk with your parents about the rules and the consequences for breaking the rules. If you believe that the consequences your parents suggest are unfair and unreasonable, tell them how you feel and why. Listen to the concern that lies behind the rules. Be respectful.

Can you suggest alternatives or compromises? Maybe your parents will agree to try things your way when you explain your reasons. If you break a rule, take responsibility for your behavior and accept the consequences. This will *really* impress your parents.

Asset #10: Parental Monitoring

GOAL: Parents who keep track of your whereabouts.

If your parents drive you crazy with questions about where you're going, who with, what for, and how long, you can do something about it. Beat them to it! Give them the information they want *before* they ask.

Another helpful hint: Put the information in the form of a question. Instead of announcing, "Tam and I are going to the 8:00 movie, then out to eat, and I'll be back before midnight," try, "I'd like to go to the 8:00 movie with Tam, then out to eat, and be back before midnight. Is that okay with you?" Then your parents can graciously give their permission. This way, everyone benefits. They get to feel generous, and you get to go out with your friend.

Asset #11: Time at Home

GOAL: Parents who limit the number of nights you can spend out of the home.

If your parents don't do this, try setting your own limits. Focus more on your school work and your family, and see if your life changes in positive ways.

For young people with jobs, spending time at home seems less important than putting in the hours at work. But when researchers at a university in Pennsylvania studied 1,800 high school students, they learned that those who work more than 15 hours a week have more problems than those who work fewer hours. Their schoolwork suffers. Their grades fall. They don't score as high on achievement tests.

You may not have a choice; you may have to work more than 15 hours a week. In this case, you're doing the best you can under the circumstances. But if you do have a choice, keep your hours to a minimum.

Asset #12: Positive Peer Influence

GOAL: Friends who are responsible, who avoid risky behaviors, and who have a positive influence on you.

Think of your three or four best friends—the people you spend the most time with and are most influenced by. Do they build you up or drag you down? Do you support one another in making good choices, even when bad choices are easily available? Only you know the answers to these questions. Forget about what your parents think or other people say. How do *you* feel about the friends you have now? If you're not happy with your answer, there are places you can go to meet new people and eventually make new friends. Ask a trusted adult (parent, teacher, youth group leader) for suggestions.

Structured Time Use

Young people need positive, constructive, interesting, and challenging things to do during their time outside of school. Boredom is a prescription for trouble. Following are ideas to try at home, at school, in the community, and in the congregation.

You'll notice that we recommend "one or more hours a week" for participation in music, extracurricular activities, and community activities, and "at least once a month" for attendance at religious programs or services. These are not intended as hard-and-fast rules, but as general guidelines. Some kids may spend only part of the year involved in music or extracurricular activities, then go on to something else for the rest of the year. All kids need to spend time at home with their families. What's important is for each family to find a balance between activities and time together—one that works for them.

ASSET #13:
Music

Kids are involved in band, orchestra, or choir, or they take music lessons. They practice one or more hours a week.

27% *of the youth we surveyed have this asset in their lives.*

At Home

▶ Encourage your kids to get involved with music as active performers. Seek out opportunities in the schools, in your community, and at your place of worship. As much as possible, let your children choose the instruments they want to play. Provide instruments and lessons. (Used instruments and group lessons are just fine.) Allow time for practice.

▶ Show your support by attending your children's performances.

▶ Don't complain when your teenager plays drums for hours (or violin, tuba, or weird noises on a synthe-sizer). If it *really* drives you crazy, take a walk or wear ear plugs.

▶ Make music a part of everyday life in your home. Explore different types of music. Be willing to listen to the music your kids enjoy—at least some of the time. For example, let them decide what station to listen to on the car radio.

▶ If you played an instrument when you were younger, consider taking a refresher course. Then set a good example and practice often. Or start learning a new instrument.

▶ Attend live music performances and concerts as a family. Scan the newspapers for notices of free performances at places of worship and community centers. Be open to a variety of experiences.

At School

▶ Provide free access to instruments to students who can't afford them. If the school can't afford them, solicit donations from parents, the community, and local businesses.

▶ When school budgets are tight, music and the arts are often among the first programs to be cut. Lobby hard to keep them at your school. Generate community support.

▶ Use music as a teaching tool in school curricula to reinforce and extend learning. Play background music during classes. While profiling famous people from history, include important musicians and play examples of their music. While exploring different cultures and languages, make music part of your lessons.

▶ Sponsor performances by local musicians and singers. Arrange for master classes, where performers share techniques and expertise with young people.

▶ Have a school talent show. Encourage soloists, groups, and garage bands to participate.

In the Community

▶ Sponsor youth bands, orchestras, and singing groups. Provide a place to practice.

▶ Provide opportunities for young people to perform in community bands or orchestras.

▶ Check with the schools to find out what they need for their music programs. Audio equipment? Tapes or CDs? Used musical instruments? Printed music? New risers for the choir? Place articles in local newspapers urging community members to contribute.

▶ Sponsor free community concerts that expose young people (and their families) to many different types of music.

▶ Promote global awareness and an appreciation for diversity by sponsoring concerts of world and ethnic music.

In the Congregation

▶ Have a youth band, choir, chorus, or other music group. Or include youth in adult groups. Some congregations are too small to have individual youth music groups; this gives kids and adults the opportunity to interact in positive ways.

▶ Instead of having a complete choir (especially during the summer months, when this sometimes proves difficult), invite members of the congregation, youth included, to perform solos, duets, or small ensemble pieces.

▶ Be open to featuring different kinds of music in your worship services. Or schedule an all-music service for one day or evening each month.

▶ Encourage adults in the congregation to offer free music lessons to young people as a ministry.

ASSET #14:

Extracurricular Activities

Kids are involved in school sports, clubs, or organizations. They participate in these extracurricular activities one or more hours a week.

61% *of the youth we surveyed have this asset in their lives.*

At Home

▶ Talk with your children about their interests. Help them to find clubs or organizations to join that match or complement their interests.

▶ Become an adult leader at your child's school. Offer to be a sponsor or adviser for an existing school club.

▶ Offer to start a new club in an area that interests you–your profession or perhaps a hobby. (An amateur astronomers' club? Photographers' club? Writers' club? Cooking club?)

▶ Start or join a car pool for kids who participate in after-school activities.

▶ Show your support by attending important club events to which parents and other adults are invited.

At School

▶ Have a system in place for informing new students and mid-year transfer students about extracurricular activities. For example, you might prepare a handout listing and describing the various clubs and after-school opportunities.

▶ Offer extracurricular activities that appeal to a wide variety of needs and interests.

In the Community

▶ Work with schools to provide extracurricular activities that are consistent with your organization's purpose. Volunteer to sponsor or lead the activities.

▶ Support school efforts to raise funds for extracurricular activities. If schools need special equipment, supplies, etc., make this public. Publish a "wish list" in the community newspaper and solicit donations.

In the Congregation

▶ Recognize that young people can excel in many areas (including sports, but not *only* sports). Publicize the various achievements of your congregation's youth in newsletters and mailings to member households.

▶ Encourage members of the congregation to volunteer as sponsors for extracurricular activities.

▶ Coordinate youth program activities so they don't conflict with important extracurricular activities. For example, if many members of your youth group play baseball in the spring, try to get copies of the practice and game schedules and work around them.

ASSET #15:

Community Activities

Kids are involved in organizations or clubs outside of school. They participate in these non-school activities one or more hours a week.

41% *of the youth we surveyed have this asset in their lives.*

At Home

▶ Survey your community to learn about activities available to young people. Watch newspapers for listings of recreational and service activities for kids. Have a family meeting to discuss the various options and to help your children choose activities that match their interests.

▶ When a child chooses an organization or club to join, suggest at least a six-month commitment. Some kids drop out of organizations prematurely, or they skip from one to another without ever giving any a chance. It takes time to really start benefiting from— and contributing to—any organization.

▶ Volunteer to sponsor, lead, or assist with a club or organization for young people. If you can't volunteer personally, contribute what you can in terms of money, materials, or services.

▶ Set a good example by getting involved in a club or organization that interests you.

▶ If you don't have time to drive your kids everywhere they need to go, there are probably other parents who feel the same. Car pool with other families so youth can participate in community activities.

At School

▶ Create a clearinghouse of community youth activities. Post information about community activities on bulletin boards along with school activities. Include important community activities in your daily announcements.

▶ Encourage students to get involved in activities outside of school. Whenever possible, combine school and community organizations and clubs.

▶ Honor school staff who contribute to the community by volunteering with organizations and clubs for kids.

▶ Coordinate with community groups so that the various opportunities available to young people meet a wide range of interests and needs.

In the Community

▶ Sponsor diverse activities to reach all youth, especially those who are underserved by existing organizations. Your criterion should not be how much a few are doing, but how many are doing something useful.

▶ Try to locate clubs and organizations on bus lines and/or in neighborhoods where the kids are. Make them inviting and accessible.

▶ Honor community members who volunteer to serve in organizations and clubs for kids. Feature stories about them in local newspapers.

▶ Gather current facts about the value and effectiveness of programs for youth. Use this information to publicize your efforts and seek community-wide support.

In the Congregation

▶ Encourage youth to get involved in community groups, as participants and as leaders.

▶ Regularly contribute to community youth organizations.

▶ Offer to sponsor an organization or club for young people, or give an existing organization a home. Many scout troops are sponsored by local congregations.

ASSET #16:

Involvement with a Faith Community

Kids regularly attend religious programs or services—at least once a month.

> **57%** *of the youth we surveyed have this asset in their lives.*

At Home

▶ As much as possible, allow your kids to share in the decision about where to attend religious services. Or, if more than one service is offered, perhaps they could choose the time.

▶ Encourage active involvement in religious activities by modeling active involvement. Don't just drop off your kids for services or classes and pick them up later.

▶ Make your faith a part of your daily life at home in whatever ways are appropriate for your family.

▶ When making important family decisions, consider them within the context of your faith.

▶ Volunteer to lead or assist with a religion class for young people.

At School

▶ Don't schedule school activities that conflict with important religious holidays, and be sure to consider the many different faith traditions within your school population (students and staff).

▶ Communicate with local religious organizations. Share holiday and activity schedules. Try to coordinate with as many as possible to avoid scheduling conflicts.

▶ If possible, incorporate information about religious holidays and traditions into class discussions. Be sure to check with your school policy first, since this is not permitted in some schools.

In the Community

▶ Don't schedule community activities that conflict with religious holidays, and be sure to consider the many different faith traditions within your community.

▶ Include religious youth workers on community-wide youth councils and task forces.

▶ Partner with local congregations in sponsoring community-wide youth events.

▶ Sponsor a series of presentations on the different faiths in your community. Invite representatives from the various religious organizations to speak. Publicize the presentations.

In the Congregation

▶ Develop strategies for your youth program that address the concerns, needs, interests, and issues of young people in your congregation.

▶ Emphasize programming that keeps youth involved in the congregation throughout high school.

▶ Include youth representation on your board.

▶ Start a suggestion box for young people. Invite them to contribute their ideas for youth activities, programs, and special events.

Tips for Teens:
Build Your Own Assets

Asset #13: Music

**GOAL: To get involved in music and spend one or
more hours a week practicing.**

Music teaches self-discipline and an appreciation for
the arts. It feels good to hear music, and it feels good
to make music. It's less important to become a great
performer than it is to enjoy and appreciate music.

If your school offers choir, band, or orchestra, get
involved. If at all possible, take private lessons on the
instrument of your choice. If you can't afford to buy an
instrument, tell your teacher. Schools with music programs often have instruments available to borrow or
rent. If that's not an option, ask for donations from
community groups. Contact local newspapers and ask
if they will write stories about your school's search for
musical instruments.

If your school doesn't offer a music program, check
with your congregation. See if your community sponsors a choir, band, or orchestra. Or start your own

band or vocal group. Many famous groups started in garages or on street corners.

Asset #14:
Extracurricular Activities

GOAL: To get involved in school sports, clubs, or organizations and spend one or more hours a week participating.

If you're not thrilled by any of the teams, clubs, or organizations offered at your school, are you sure that you've checked into all of them? You may find a special interest group you enjoy. If not, think about starting one. Find 5–10 students who share your interest, then get together and talk about the kind of group you'd like to start. Once you have defined your purpose, decided on a few goals, and outlined some possible activities, approach a teacher you like and ask him or her to sponsor you.

Asset #15: Community Activities

GOAL: To get involved in organizations or clubs outside of school and spend one or more hours a week participating.

Check with your community center, local arts organization, religious organization, and civic groups to learn what's available. You'll find groups especially for young people, and groups of adults that welcome young people. If you don't find something that interests you, post messages on bulletin boards. You'll find other people who share your interests, and you can decide together what to do next.

Asset #16: Involvement with a Faith Community

GOAL: To attend religious programs or services at least once a month.

Your congregation can be a source of support, encouragement, and affirmation throughout your life. A faith community of caring people who share similar values and views can be a good place to find adults to talk to—just what you need to build assets #4 and #5.

Many kids drop out of their congregations as teenagers. Religion—or organized religion—no longer seems relevant to their lives. Their parents may want them to keep attending services, but they get so tired of arguing that they eventually give up and stop making them go. If you feel that your congregation is out of touch with young people, don't drop out. Speak up. Talk with the people who lead the youth program. Come with ideas and offer to help. Suggest a round-table discussion—an opportunity for young people to express their opinions, thoughts, and needs.

Don't just expect your congregation to serve you. What can you contribute? For example, if you would like your place of worship to offer one service a month especially for young people, maybe you could help to organize it. The more involved you become, the more meaningful the experience will be for you, and the less likely you are to walk away.

If your parents aren't involved in a faith community, this doesn't mean that you can't be. Perhaps you can join a friend's congregation. Or visit the congregations in your neighborhood or nearby. Talk with the people who lead the youth program and explain that you're looking for a faith community to join.

What if your parents are involved in a faith community, but their choice doesn't seem right for you? Try to talk with them about the way you feel. Maybe they will agree to help you find a community that meets your spiritual needs.

Building
Internal Assets

Educational Commitment

Young people need to believe that a good education is important to their lives. They need to feel motivated to do well in school and continue their education. Following are inspiring ideas for building children's commitment to education at home, at school, in the community, and in the congregation.

ASSET #17:

Achievement Motivation

Kids are motivated to learn and do their best in school.

> **70%** *of the youth we surveyed have this asset in their lives.*

At Home

▶ Be a role model for lifelong learning. Show an ongoing interest in learning new things and making new discoveries.

▶ Learn along with your children. Go someplace new together and explore. Read the same books and discuss them afterward, or take turns choosing books for everyone to read. Take a community education class together. Brainstorm a list of questions you're all curious about, then visit the library to find the answers.

▶ Encourage your kids to do their best at school, but don't expect perfection, and leave plenty of room for mistakes.

▶ If your kids seem apathetic about school or resist going to school, try to find out why. Is school too easy for them, or too hard? Are they getting the help and support they need? Do they feel safe at school? Talk with their teachers. Do what you can to change things, working with other parents and school staff— or switch schools.

At School

▶ Relate lesson content and curricula to real-life situations and issues. Use enrichment materials.

▶ People learn in different ways. Train teachers to recognize and teach to various learning styles, and to value the many different kinds of intelligence.

▶ Affirm and encourage achievement in diverse areas as students discover their own interests and capabilities.

▶ Personal attention and interest from a teacher can be a powerful motivator. Encourage teachers to get to know their students.

In the Community

▶ Make sure that your programming for youth is enjoyable, meaningful, *and* intellectually challenging. Sponsor trips to museums, exhibits, films, lectures, etc.

▶ Encourage young people to use what they're learning in school to address issues in your program. For example, if they have been studying cultural diversity, they might have good suggestions for making your program more inclusive.

▶ Put motivated, achieving high school students together with younger kids on community projects. The older kids might inspire the younger ones.

▶ Start a Speakers' Bureau of high achievers in your community–including both adults and students. Publicize their availability to speak at area schools.

In the Congregation

▶ Affirm the value of education in all youth programming. Even if you disagree with the way a particular subject is being taught, address only that subject; don't undermine education as a whole.

▶ Make school a regular topic of conversation in youth groups.

▶ Make youth programming intellectually challenging. Help young people to see, appreciate, and think about the complexities in faith, theology, and ethics. Affirm kids who ask tough questions. When appropriate, have them apply skills they learn in school to the content of your youth program.

ASSET #18:
Educational Aspiration

Kids hope and plan to pursue their
education beyond high school, either
in college or in trade school.

89% *of the youth we surveyed
have this asset in their lives.*

At Home

▶ Talk with your kids about life goals, priorities, and
dreams. The question you ask when they're very
young—"What do you want to be when you grow
up?"—can gradually be expanded to "How can you
become what you want to be? What steps can you
take?"

▶ Commit to helping support your teen through post-
high-school education. Work with a financial
planner to start saving now.

▶ Be a role model for continuing education. Take
classes and courses at your local college or through
community education.

▶ Many colleges offer summer programs for junior high
and high school students. Gather information on
summer programs and help your kids choose those
that interest them. Early exposure to a college setting
can inspire them and ease some of their anxieties.

▶ Encourage your kids to start gathering information on various colleges during the first years of high school—even in junior high. Suggest that they do a mini-research project: Identify one or two strong areas of interest, then locate colleges that offer strong programs in those areas.

At School

▶ Assign classroom projects that involve researching educational possibilities.

▶ Keep current files on colleges, universities, and pro-fessional schools in your city and state, as well as nationwide and international programs. Include information about financial aid. Make the files accessible to students.

▶ Invite students from local colleges and trade schools to speak to your classes.

▶ Make college recruiters welcome at your school, and give students time to meet with them.

▶ Make military recruiters welcome at your school, too. For many kids, military service is an excellent option for after high school—and a way to help pay for college later.

▶ Sponsor career days. Invite parents and other people from your community to speak to student groups about their careers. Allow time for them to meet with individual students to answer questions and offer guidance and suggestions.

In the Community

▶ Include college and career issues in your services and programming. You might sponsor a series of workshops on finding the right college, filling out college applications, and locating sources of financial aid.

▶ Offer mentoring programs that match youth with adults from a variety of careers. Encourage the adults to serve as volunteer leaders in other community programs.

▶ Invite representatives from local colleges and trade schools to speak at community meetings.

In the Congregation

▶ Take high school students on a spring break tour of colleges in your state or neighboring states that are affiliated with your faith tradition.

▶ Provide opportunities for youth to talk about their future choices from a faith perspective.

▶ Start a scholarship fund.

▶ Survey members to find out what colleges or professional schools they attended. See if they would be willing to meet with young people to offer advice and answer questions.

ASSET #19:

School Performance

Kids do well in school. Their grades are above average.

47% *of the youth we surveyed have this asset in their lives.*

At Home

▶ Affirm school success through family celebrations. The student who goes from a D to a C in science deserves to be celebrated as much as the student who always brings home straight A's.

▶ Stay in contact with teachers about your children's progress. Don't wait for report cards.

▶ Post student awards, report cards, honor roll lists, and other signs of achievement prominently in your home. Attend awards ceremonies and graduations.

▶ Treat each of your children as individuals and value their achievements individually. Don't compare your kids' school performance.

▶ Make it known that you value good grades but you don't expect perfection. Many kids go through a "slump" at some point during their school career. Don't panic! Instead, keep offering support and encouragement.

At School

▶ Expect students to do well and encourage parents to expect the same.

▶ Don't assume that kids know how to study. Teach basic study skills and review them periodically.

▶ Hold awards ceremonies that honor all kinds of achievers, from the student who gets good grades to the student who is voted "most eager to learn" by teachers. Invite parents to attend.

▶ Invite parents and other adults in the community to tutor students who need extra help.

In the Community

▶ Affirm and recognize success in school. Post the names of honor students on community center bulletin boards and publish them in local newspapers.

▶ Offer evening and weekend classes for kids on basic study skills.

▶ Encourage community members to volunteer as tutors.

In the Congregation

▶ Recognize good school performance. Publish the names of achieving students in your worship bulletin.

▶ Provide opportunities for youth to be tutors for younger children. If this turns out to be successful, consider expanding it into a community outreach program.

ASSET #20:

Homework

Kids regularly spend time doing homework. They do six or more hours of homework a week.

24% *of the youth we surveyed have this asset in their lives.*

At Home

▶ Provide a quiet, comfortable, well-lit place for your kids to study without distractions.

▶ Turn off the television and limit the number of hours your teen can spend at an after-school job.

▶ Work with your child to set up a regular homework schedule, then respect it. Arrange dinner and family events around the homework schedule.

▶ If homework time comes before dinner, make healthy snacks available. Hungry kids have trouble concentrating.

▶ Be available to answer questions, drill on vocabulary words, check homework, offer support, etc.

▶ Help your child to prioritize homework assignments. (It's best to do the hard ones *first*—to get them out of the way before fatigue sets in.) Work with your child to plan long-term assignments.

At School

▶ Regularly assign homework and hold students accountable for completing it.

▶ Communicate with other teachers about homework, test schedules, and long-term assignments. Spread them out evenly over the year so students aren't swamped.

▶ Make homework relevant to other parts of students' lives—family, work, hobbies, community.

▶ Set up a homework hotline staffed by teachers, other adults, and older students.

In the Community

▶ Arrange after-school study programs. Set aside a quiet room for kids to do their homework, read, study for tests, etc. Staff it with adult volunteers from the community.

▶ Expect young people to complete their homework as a requirement for participating in activities and programs. You won't be able to monitor this, but you can ask kids if they are keeping up with their homework and encourage them to do so. If enough adults express interest and concern, this becomes a community standard.

▶ Schedule a "homework hour" before after-school or evening activities.

▶ Set up a homework hotline staffed by volunteers from the community. Encourage the local high school to adopt this as a service project and give students service credits for working the hotline on school nights and weekends. Provide resources:

telephones, desks and tables, dictionaries, computers, reference works, etc.

In the Congregation

▶ Reduce conflicts between time commitments for religious activities and homework. Try not to overschedule youth group members during the school year. Plan weeknight activities for later in the evening, after homework is finished.

▶ Set up a homework hotline staffed by adults and high school students from the congregation.

▶ Open the youth room after school as a study and homework center. Staff it with adult volunteers

Tips for Teens:
Build Your Own Assets

Asset #17: Achievement
Motivation

GOAL: To feel motivated to learn and do your best in school.

Do you feel as if school is a waste of your time? Then do something about it. Take charge of your own education. Set goals for yourself, ask questions in class, and find an ally—a teacher or school counselor who can help you to get more out of school. Also, consider your friends' attitudes toward school. If you're spending most of your time with kids who hate school and do the minimum work needed to pass, maybe you need new friends.

Asset #18: Educational Aspiration

GOAL: To continue your education beyond high school.

What are your goals for the future? What do you see yourself doing as an adult? Chances are, you'll need to go to college or trade school to realize your goals. It's never too soon to start gathering information on colleges and professional schools. Contact the ones that look interesting to you and ask for the names of graduates who live in your area. Then talk to the people who have gone to the schools. You'll gain valuable information and insight, and you might also find a friend—someone who will write you a glowing recommendation when the time comes.

If you're not clear about the kind of school you'd like to attend, work with a school counselor. He or she can help you to clarify your interests, assess your abilities and skills, and identify appropriate schools to consider.

Asset #19: School Performance

GOAL: To earn grades that are above average or better.

Good grades are your ticket to college and professional school admission, scholarships, financial aid, and other important steps toward achieving your goals. If your grades could use some help, see what's available at your school. Can you get a tutor? Can you ask your teachers for tips on raising your grades?

Often, grades are a combination of factors: assignments done, papers turned in on time, test scores, class participation. Don't make the mistake of skipping assignments or turning papers in a day late. What seems to you like an insignificant little worksheet can affect your final grade.

Asset #20: Homework

GOAL: To spend six or more hours a week on homework.

Make homework your first priority—before favorite TV programs, time with your friends, extracurricular activities, even a job. What if you don't have six hours of homework in a typical week? Spend the time reading more about a particular subject, practicing your skills, or reviewing your books and notes. It's vital to form the homework habit now, especially if you plan to go to college.

Positive Values

Young people need a strong inner core of positive values—beliefs and convictions that guide their decisions and behaviors. These values include a sense of personal responsibility for the welfare of others and a commitment to honoring themselves. Following are ideas for helping children form and strengthen their values at home, at school, in the community, and in the congregation.

ASSET #21:
Helping People

**Kids believe that it is important to help other
people and work to improve their lives.**

52% *of the youth we surveyed
have this asset in their lives.*

At Home

▶ Regularly spend family time helping others.
Volunteer at your local food shelf, at shelters or
soup kitchens for homeless people, at nursing
homes. It's tremendously inspiring for kids to see
their parents helping others and to know that they
as children can make a difference, too.

▶ Show care and concern for your neighbors. Is there
an elderly person who needs help with shopping and
home maintenance? Someone who could use a
hand with yard work? Set a good example and get
your kids involved.

▶ Have family meetings to brainstorm ways of helping
people. Decide together that you will spend a certain
number of hours each week being of service to
others.

▶ Instead of spending money on holiday gifts for each
other, identify a family in need. (Ask at your child's
school, at your community center, and/or at your
place of worship.) Then work together as a family to

compile a list of gifts and necessities and shop for them. Arrange to have everything delivered anonymously.

▶ Establish an atmosphere of mutual caring and helpfulness within your home.

▶ Encourage and support your teen to help other people, even when it feels uncomfortable or risky. For example, it may seem risky to do a clean-up project in a high-crime neighborhood, but if appropriate precautions are taken, the benefits for everyone can far outweigh the risks.

At School

▶ Encourage all students to participate in service activities or service-learning classes. Give credits, not grades, for participation. Work with your community to learn where students can be of the most service, then provide a range of options.

▶ Provide cooperative learning opportunities for all students. The brightest students shouldn't always be the ones who are helping others. Work with your less able students to identify their special talents and abilities so they can be helpers, too.

▶ Create a peer counseling program in your school. Train students to be good listeners, to guide their peers in resolving problems and making decisions, and to know when to seek help from adults.

▶ Honor and affirm students who help others. Give special awards and recognition for service.

▶ Honor and affirm school staff who are active in community service. Promote them as role models. Start a mentoring program to match students with caring staff.

In the Community

▶ Include service projects and reflection as an integral part of all youth programming.

▶ Work closely with your community to identify opportunities for young people to serve others. Invite youth to brainstorm service ideas.

▶ Honor and affirm youth who serve others. Sponsor an annual awards celebration and publicize it in local newspapers.

▶ Identify community members who are active in serving others. Invite them to speak to young people. Encourage them to mentor young people who also want to serve.

▶ Form relationships with national service organizations. Invite representatives to speak in your community. Encourage community members–youth and adults–to volunteer with the organizations of their choice.

▶ Teach youth caring skills and provide ample opportunities to use them within the community.

In the Congregation

▶ Include peer ministry in your youth programming.

▶ Make young people aware of the service opportunities available within your congregation. Announce them during worship services. Provide opportunities for kids and adults to serve together.

▶ Make youth aware of service opportunities in the community.

▶ Invite young people to contribute their own ideas for helping others.

▶ Honor and affirm members of all ages who help others and try to improve their lives.

Asset #22:

Global Concern

Kids are concerned about global issues such as the environment, world peace, violence prevention, and world hunger.

> **47%** *of the youth we surveyed have this asset in their lives.*

At Home

▶ Gather information about charitable organizations. Have a family discussion to decide which one(s) your family will help to support. Encourage everyone to contribute. Young children can set aside part of their allowance; older kids can chip in a portion of their earnings from jobs and chores.

▶ Instead of spending money on holiday gifts, make a family contribution to a charitable organization.

▶ Talk with your children about world disasters and countries where people are suffering. Watch news programs, read newspapers, and visit the library for more information. Is there something that touches your children personally? A war, famine, earthquake, or flood? Find a way for your family to help. For example, newspapers often publish the names, addresses, and telephone numbers of international relief organizations following major events.

▶ Take family vacations in which you expose your kids firsthand to communities in need. For example, if you visit Washington, D.C., on vacation, don't just focus on the glamorous and exciting places. Also learn about areas of the city with serious problems. Visit museums that address issues of justice and equality.

At School

▶ Include global concerns in class discussions and curricula. Assign research projects on current issues and events.

▶ Invite representatives from international service, relief, and human rights organizations to speak to students. If possible, have small group discussions so students and adults can interact one-on-one.

▶ Offer a unit of study on people who have made a difference in the world through activism and service.

▶ Sponsor school-wide emphases on particular global concerns, then address them in all areas of the curriculum.

In the Community

▶ Give young people responsibility and leadership for service projects. Let them prove to themselves that they can make a difference.

▶ Sponsor community discussions about global concerns. Invite representatives from service and relief organizations to speak. Schedule the discussions for a time when kids can attend with their parents.

▶ Post fact sheets about global issues on bulletin boards. Have brochures available from service and relief organizations.

▶ Always take time to talk with young people after they have completed service projects. This helps them to understand the issues and make important connections between their actions and how they affect others.

In the Congregation

▶ Include global issues in youth programming. Sponsor discussions and arrange ways for youth to get involved.

▶ Address global issues in sermons, homilies, and messages to the congregation.

▶ Invite young people to contribute their ideas when planning ways for your congregation to address global concerns.

▶ Through trips, speakers, service projects, and simulations, make world issues personally relevant to youth.

▶ Honor and affirm members who volunteer or work for service and relief organizations.

ASSET #23:

Empathy

Kids care about other people's feelings.

86% *of the youth we surveyed have this asset in their lives.*

At Home

▶ Model mutual respect in the family. Do not tolerate put-downs, insults, name-calling, or bullying from *any* family member.

▶ Remember that what seems trivial to an adult can be terribly important to a child. Practice seeing things from a child's perspective. Then you can truly empathize when your kids come to you with problems or concerns. They, in turn, will learn to empathize with others.

▶ Watch videos as a family that show people caring about each other. Talk about what motivates people to express concern for others.

▶ When you see people in difficult situations, work with your kids to understand some of the person's feelings and experience. For example, if you see a homeless person, help your children to think about what it might be like not to have a place to live.

▶ When your children do things that are selfish or hurt other people's feelings, talk with them about how their choices and behaviors affect other people.

At School

▶ Teach students conflict resolution skills. Train them to solve problems calmly and creatively while respecting the feelings of everyone involved.

▶ Hold discussion groups about social and emotional experiences during lunch or after school. Encourage students to talk about their feelings and explore appropriate ways to express them.

▶ Expose students to the life experiences of other people in concrete ways. Tie this to the curriculum. For example, when discussing the 1960s in history class, invite a civil rights activist to describe the experience.

▶ Expect everyone at school to show respect and concern for one another—staff and students. Do not tolerate put-downs, insults, name-calling, or bullying.

▶ Use role-playing and creative visualization exercises to teach empathy and respect for other people's feelings.

In the Community

▶ Emphasize cooperation over competition in activities and games.

▶ Take time to listen to kids express their feelings. Encourage them to listen to one another.

▶ Seek to include a diversity of kids (economic, ethnic, religious) in programs so all young people are exposed to others whose experiences are different from theirs.

In the Congregation

▶ Give youth opportunities to share their feelings in "safe" groups of supportive peers with an adult leader who is attentive and respectful.

▶ Use role-playing and other techniques to help young people see issues from different perspectives.

▶ Sponsor service projects and mission trips that bring youth into contact with different cultures and traditions. Take time to reflect on the experiences so kids will internalize the feelings of empathy.

▶ Model empathy and respect for one another's feelings within your congregation.

ASSET #24:
Sexual Restraint

Kids believe that it is important to abstain from sex. They are willing to postpone becoming sexually active.

> **36%** *of the youth we surveyed have this asset in their lives.*

At Home

▶ Talk openly with your kids about sex—or as openly as you can. If you're painfully uncomfortable discussing certain aspects, be honest about it and provide age-appropriate books.

▶ Share with your kids your personal values about why it's important for teenagers not to be sexually active. Help them to see how your beliefs shape your actions and priorities.

▶ Make your family's expectations clear. Many parents clearly express their expectations about alcohol and other drug use, drinking and driving, etc., but they hesitate to say, "We expect you not to have sex while you're a teenager." Young people need to hear this from their parents.

▶ Encourage your teenagers to make a commitment not to have sex while they're still in school. More and more teenagers are choosing to abstain, and some are going public with their decision. They are finding that this frees them from the sexual pressures other kids experience.

▶ If you learn that your teenagers are already sexually active, encourage them to reevaluate their choice in light of values that are important to them. For example, if they strongly believe in justice, talk about how having sex too early often exploits one person in the relationship.

▶ Teach and model appropriate ways to show affection.

At School

▶ Whether schools should teach sex education remains a matter of debate. This is something your school will need to decide within the context of your community. If you do teach sex education, use a values-based curriculum that helps kids sort out their values and understand how those values shape their behaviors.

▶ Train peer counselors to affirm young people who choose abstinence.

▶ Give students opportunities to express their values, attitudes, and concerns about sex.

▶ Make appropriate resources (books, videos) available in the media center.

In the Community

▶ Have clear expectations of how youth should relate to one another in all activities.

▶ Create a climate in which abstinence by youth is valued and affirmed.

▶ Invite community health professionals to speak about teenagers and sex.

▶ Talk about how community norms either encourage kids to be sexually abstinent or discourage them from making this choice. For example, do young people have easy access to sexually explicit movies, videos, and magazines? If so, what can your community do to limit or restrict their access to such materials?

In the Congregation

▶ Include discussions of sexual values in your religious education programming. Clearly communicate what your faith tradition teaches about sex and sexual behavior.

▶ Find ways for youth to affirm and support each other in making positive choices about sex. Help them articulate the reasons for their decisions.

▶ Invite young people to make a commitment not to have sex during their teenage years. If appropriate, they can do this publicly; if not, privately.

▶ Even if teenagers have been sexually active, encourage and affirm decisions to stop. Talk with sexually active teens about important values they can build by refraining from sexual activity.

Tips for Teens: Build Your Own Assets

Asset #21: Helping People

GOAL: To help other people and work to improve their lives.

There are many opportunities within your community to reach out and help others. There are countless examples of young people who have made a difference in people's lives. Start by choosing a problem you'd like to help solve—something that personally interests you. Do your research, enlist friends to help, brainstorm ideas, and get started.

Asset #22: Global Concern

GOAL: To be concerned about global issues such as the environment, world peace, violence prevention, and world hunger.

Each one of us is a citizen of the world. Communication technology has made it possible to stay on top of news from almost everywhere. Turn on CNN, listen to public radio, read newspapers and magazines. If you have a computer and a modem, connect to the Internet. Educate yourself about the world's people and problems. You can't stop a war or save a nation, but you can do something. Help to support a relief organization or human rights organization. Join a letter-writing campaign. Volunteer your time at a service organization or through your congregation. Every effort, however small it may seem, has the potential to profoundly change someone's life. It will surely change yours.

Asset #23: Empathy

GOAL: To care about other people's feelings.

Empathy begins by determining how you want to be treated—probably with kindness and respect. From there, it's not too hard to understand that other people want to be treated the same. If you remember times when you were treated unkindly, even cruelly, you can make a personal decision not to say or do things that will cause pain to others.

It's very difficult to be empathetic from a distance. Take time to get to know people—especially people who are different from you. Find opportunities to care for or support them. Listen to their stories. Before judging them for their choices or circumstances, find out more information about their values, beliefs, and priorities.

Asset #24: Sexual Restraint

GOAL: To abstain from sex as a teenager; to postpone becoming sexually active.

Kids are becoming sexually active at increasingly younger ages. You've probably read stories about boys who are fathers at 13 or 14, girls who are pregnant at 11 or 12. You've also heard about AIDS and other sexually transmitted diseases. It's scary out there, and you are not exempt.

Sex is so tempting. Sexual pressure can be almost irresistible. Especially if your friends are sexually active, you may feel left out if you aren't, too. If you're a boy, you may think that you have to prove yourself by having sex. If you're a girl, you may feel that the only way to keep a boy interested is to have sex with him. Or you may decide that you want someone in your life who really belongs to you—like a baby.

The fact is, sex is the *last* thing you need right now. What you need is to finish high school, continue your education, and get ready for life as an adult. You need to develop healthy, caring, mutually respectful relationships before encountering all of the complications that come with sexual involvement. You don't need the distraction, the emotional ups and downs, and the potential life-changing consequences of sex.

Your choice about sex says a lot about your personal values. Not having sex is a powerful way to show that you can control yourself, that you respect other people, and that you're not going to make promises you can't keep. *If you've already had sex, you can stop now and develop those same values.*

You have the power to make one of the most important decisions in your life: to not have sex—or to stop having sex—until you're really ready. Young people who have chosen to abstain report that it's a big relief. You may want to try it and see for yourself.

Social Competencies

Part of growing up involves developing skills and attitudes—social competencies—that help one function as an independent, competent person. Young people need to know how to be assertive, make decisions, make friends, and plan ahead. They also need a strong sense of positive self-esteem and a feeling of hope for the future. Following are ideas for helping children form and strengthen these social competencies at home, at school, in the community, and in the congregation.

ASSET #25:
Assertiveness Skills

Kids can stick up for themselves and their beliefs.

83% *of the youth we surveyed have this asset in their lives.*

At Home

▶ Teach your kids the difference between assertiveness, aggression, and passivity. Assertiveness is positive and affirming; aggression is negative and demanding; passivity makes one vulnerable. Role-play all three kinds of behavior with your children.

▶ Point out assertive, aggressive, and passive behaviors you see in movies, videos, and television programs you watch together.

▶ Find out what your kids believe by asking them. If they have trouble articulating their beliefs, offer to help, but don't put words in their mouths. Listen to what they have to say. Try not to be too alarmed if some of their beliefs clash with yours; this is perfectly normal. Don't criticize.

▶ Teach your kids to stick up for themselves instead of just going along with the crowd because it's easier. Have them practice being assertive with seemingly inconsequential issues. This builds skills for the tough times.

▶ Role-play situations in which someone challenges your children's beliefs. What do your children say? Can they stick up for themselves? If they don't know what to say, offer suggestions.

▶ Tell your kids what you believe. Tell them about times when you've had to stick up for your beliefs in the face of opposition. Call their attention to beliefs you have in common with them. Give them permission to have their own beliefs.

At School

▶ Encourage students to express their beliefs verbally and in writing without fear of being put down.

▶ Create an environment in which students and staff respect the right of every individual to have his or her own beliefs.

▶ Encourage students to stick up for themselves when others take advantage of them.

▶ Teach the difference between assertiveness, aggression, and passivity. Model and role-play assertiveness skills.

▶ As a classroom or even a school-wide project, invite students to write statements of their beliefs. Combine them on a ballot and have students vote for their top five. Recast them as "We believe..." and post them as a school creed.

▶ Show that you value assertiveness in your interactions with students—in the classroom, in teacher-student conferences, and on other occasions. Be willing to listen even when you disagree.

In the Community

▶ Provide opportunities for young people to act on their values and beliefs.

▶ Make it clear that people within your community are not to be devalued or criticized because of what they believe.

▶ Model an appreciation for diversity and a tolerance for differences.

▶ Encourage young people to attend meetings about important community issues. These usually attract people with differing views who are there to speak up and be heard. Kids will see first-hand how people stick up for their beliefs, and they may want to assert their own positions as well.

In the Congregation

▶ Give youth opportunities to express their beliefs— even beliefs that are not well-formed, and even beliefs that are not commonly held by your congregation or your faith tradition.

▶ Start a discussion group for young people. Encourage them to talk about controversial topics. Set group rules: no put-downs, no criticism, and everyone has the chance to contribute.

▶ It's common for adolescents to challenge the beliefs of their faith tradition. Adult leaders need to know when to listen and when to calmly reinforce the beliefs of the faith tradition.

ASSET #26:
Decision-Making Skills

**Kids know how to make decisions.
They are good at making positive decisions.**

69% *of the youth we surveyed
have this asset in their lives.*

At Home

▶ Include your kids in family decisions that affect
them. Give them a chance to talk, and listen respectfully. Consider their feelings and opinions when
making decisions.

▶ Model the decision-making process for your kids:
gathering information, viewing the decision from all
sides, weighing consequences, listing pros and cons,
making a choice and sticking to it. Help them apply
this process to a decision they must make.

▶ Point out that not making a decision *is* making a
decision: it's deciding not to decide. Explain that
this gives someone else the power to determine what
happens next.

▶ Allow for mistakes. Don't blow up at a poor decision.
Instead, help your kids learn from it. Don't protect
them from the consequences of poor decisions.

▶ Encourage your kids to keep a journal of decisions and consequences. Explain that they should write down what happened *and* how they felt at the time. This serves as positive reinforcement for good decisions, and as a strong reminder of the effects of bad decisions.

At School

▶ Challenge students to articulate the reasons behind their decisions. This helps students to see both the strengths and the flaws in their decision-making process.

▶ Include student leaders on decision-making committees and boards.

▶ Assign projects that build decision-making skills.

▶ Ask students to talk about or write about tough decisions they have had to make.

In the Community

▶ Permit young people to participate in decision-making about programs and special projects.

▶ Use experiential activities and simulations that challenge youth to make difficult decisions.

▶ Invite speakers to talk to kids about important decisions they have made.

▶ Train adult leaders in helping kids through the decision-making process. They might be available to offer guidance or simply to listen.

In the Congregation

▶ Let young people make decisions about the direction of the youth program.

▶ Include students in decision-making that affects the congregation as a whole.

▶ When appropriate, point out to youth how their faith informs their decisions.

▶ Include young people on decision-making committees and task forces that affect the lives of youth in the community.

ASSET #27:
Friendship-Making Skills

**Kids know how to make and keep friends.
They are good at forming positive friendships.**

> **75%** *of the youth we surveyed
> have this asset in their lives.*

At Home

▶ Model the importance of friendship in your own life.
Invite your friends to your home. Do things with
your friends that also include your kids so they can
get to know one another. Take family vacations with
your friends and their families.

▶ If your kids have few or no friends, try to find out
why. Do they need help initiating friendships? Do
they know how to meet people, start conversations,
and ask questions to indicate their interest in
others? These are skills you can practice at home.

▶ Some kids don't fit in with other kids their age. This
is often the case with bright kids, or kids who just
march to the beat of a different drummer. Try to find
other opportunities for your child to make friends–
groups that include both younger and older kids,
hobby clubs, service organizations, community
groups.

▶ Emphasize the value of diversity in friendships. Encourage your kids to form friendships with people of different ages, ethnic origins, cultural backgrounds, and faiths. Try to set an example by your own choice of friends.

▶ Help your children come up with ideas for fun and creative things to do with their friends. Offer to drive, rent videos, make popcorn, etc.

▶ Encourage your kids to invite their friends to your home.

At School

▶ Use teaching styles that promote interaction and friendship-building among students.

▶ Mix students in groups that reflect the diversity of your school. Kids who form friendships are less likely to develop prejudices.

▶ Be aware of friendships among your students and alert to sudden changes. For example, if you notice that two "best friends" stop speaking, you might facilitate a meeting that brings them back together.

▶ Talk about the importance of friendship in your life. Share stories and anecdotes about your friends, things you've done together, and why your friends mean so much to you.

▶ Help new students to fit in. Ask them about their interests, and introduce them to other students who share their interests.

In the Community

▶ Challenge youth to reach out to newcomers and others who may not have friends.

▶ Watch how young people interact with each other, and identify those who may need special help with friendship skills. Train adult leaders to teach friendship skills.

▶ For activities, service projects, and special programs, mix young people in groups that reflect the diversity of your community.

▶ Provide ample opportunities for young people to widen their circle of friends.

In the Congregation

▶ Start a discussion group on dating, making and keeping friends, and other relationship issues.

▶ Give youth opportunities to get to know people who are different from them. Talk with them about the challenges in those relationships.

▶ Plan social events to which young people may invite friends from outside the congregation.

▶ Be a friendly congregation. Help new people and visitors feel welcome and accepted.

ASSET #28:
Planning Skills

Kids know how to plan ahead.

59% *of the youth we surveyed have this asset in their lives.*

At Home

▶ Have family meetings to talk about future plans that affect all family members. Work together to set priorities. Invite suggestions from everyone, even the youngest children.

▶ Give your kids responsibility for planning certain family events. For example, they could plan and prepare dinner one night a week. A child who loves maps might plan part of a family car trip.

▶ Give your children daily planners or date books. Demonstrate how to use them. Help them to form the habit of making and prioritizing things-to-do lists.

▶ Ask your kids to tell you when they receive long-term assignments—papers, projects, reports. Offer to help them plan ahead so they're not overwhelmed at the last minute.

▶ Give your teenagers more and more responsibility for planning their own future. This might include saving money for a special purchase or finding a summer job before school ends. Prompt good planning by asking questions, but don't take over the planning process.

At School

▶ Let students plan class projects and assignments, even school-wide activities.

▶ Teach planning and organizational skills. Include them in assignments. For example, when you assign a research paper, also assign a series of due dates for the various steps involved–choosing a theme, going to the library, preparing an outline, writing a first draft, revising, etc.

▶ Create assignment sheets to copy and give your students. Or, if possible, provide students with planners for the school year.

▶ Train staff in helping students make long-term plans for continuing their education and choosing a career.

In the Community

▶ Have youth identify something in the community they would like to change, then develop two or three plans for changing it. If a plan seems feasible, put it into action.

▶ Offer workshops for community members on planning and organization skills.

In the Congregation

▶ Give young people an active role in planning the youth program. For example, if kids really want a basketball court on the parking lot, help them to think about everything they would have to do to make it happen.

▶ Include youth in congregation-wide planning meetings and groups so they can learn from others.

▶ Invite kids to plan special events. Even young children can do this with adult guidance and supervision.

ASSET #29:

Self-Esteem

**Kids have positive self-esteem.
They feel good about themselves.**

47% *of the youth we surveyed
have this asset in their lives.*

At Home

▶ Express your love for your children regularly and often. Show them and tell them every day.

▶ Celebrate each child's uniqueness. Find something special to value and affirm, whether it's a sense of humor, computer skills, singing voice, or wonderful smile.

▶ When your kids make mistakes or bad choices, separate the deed from the doer. The choice is bad, not the child.

▶ Treat your children with respect. Listen without interrupting; talk without yelling.

▶ When they ask for something and you say no, try to give a reasonable explanation for your decision. This is common courtesy.

▶ Encourage your kids to keep a journal of their accomplishments. This eventually becomes a "savings account" of positive feelings.

At School

▶ Use grading as an opportunity to affirm. This doesn't mean giving students grades they don't deserve. Instead, grade honestly, then add positive comments.

▶ Critique papers, reports, and tests constructively. Offer suggestions for improvements. Add positive comments.

▶ Teach students to accept criticism and respond in constructive ways.

▶ Treat all students with respect. Encourage everyone to contribute to class discussions. Identify and affirm individual talents.

In the Community

▶ Take time to pay attention to every young person— for example, while waiting in line at the grocery store or the movie theater. Demonstrate by your attitude and behavior that you value them and enjoy talking with them.

▶ Offer classes and workshops for young people on developing and strengthening self-esteem. Topics might include positive self-talk, learning from mistakes, accepting compliments, and asking for what they need.

▶ Invite experts to speak to parents about building self-esteem in children.

In the Congregation

▶ Accept and affirm all young people for who they are. Recognize and affirm individual talents, abilities, and accomplishments.

▶ Hold a workshop for parents on building self-esteem in their children.

▶ Feature brief biographies in the worship bulletin of young people who belong to your congregation.

ASSET #30:

Hope

Kids have a positive view of their personal future. They are generally optimistic about their lives.

> **69%** *of the youth we surveyed have this asset in their lives.*

At Home

▶ Inspire hope by being hopeful. Look forward to your own future and the future of your family.

▶ Don't dismiss your children's dreams as naive or unrealistic. Instead, encourage them to tell you their dreams. Share in their enthusiasm. Help them make plans to realize their dreams.

▶ Eliminate pessimistic phrases from your family vocabulary. Replace "It won't work" with "Why not try it?" Instead of "You can't do that by yourself," try "I can help you."

▶ Pay particular attention to signs of hope in your community and world. Don't just focus on all of the things that are wrong about the present or scary about the future.

▶ Take time to enjoy life. Notice and appreciate a beautiful sunset, a good dinner, a funny show on television, a flower in your garden, a song heard on the car radio. Share your joy with your children.

▶ Be spontaneous. Drop everything to play ball, take a walk, catch a movie, or play a game with your kids. Spontaneity is essentially hopeful; you choose to do something suddenly because you expect to have a good time.

At School

▶ Encourage and support students in pursuing their dreams.

▶ Expose students to positive role models whose backgrounds are similar to theirs. This is especially important for students who come from troubled or economically disadvantaged families. It gives them hope for their own future.

▶ Create a climate of optimism. Expect your students to succeed. Even a poor grade can be accompanied by an encouraging note: "I know you'll do better next time if you try."

In the Community

▶ Help young people to set personal goals that inspire hope.

▶ Encourage kids to name their fears—things that might stop them from reaching their goals. Once fears are named, they can be addressed and dealt with.

▶ Affirm and publicize the good things about your community. Be optimistic about its future.

In the Congregation

▶ Encourage kids to talk about their hopes and dreams.

▶ Pass on to young people the hope that is integral to your faith tradition.

▶ Do projects that point to a more hopeful future. Instead of always addressing problems, identify areas of hope, creativity, and new life and encourage kids to get involved.

Tips for Teens:
Build Your Own Assets

Asset #25: Assertiveness Skills

GOAL: To be able to stick up for your own beliefs.

What are your beliefs? Have you ever thought about this? Take a few minutes to make a list. Start each item with "I believe...." This will help you to articulate your beliefs. Then read your list, make any changes, and keep revising until it feels right to you. Now you know what to stick up for.

    Don't wait until you're in a tough situation to assert yourself. Do it earlier, when the stakes aren't as high. For example, when you're trying to choose a movie with your friends, speak up about the one you really want to see.

Asset #26: Decision-Making Skills

GOAL: To be good at making decisions.

Does it seem as if your parents make a lot of the decisions, including some you'd like to make yourself? Ask if you can start making some decisions. If you prove that you're responsible, your parents will have more confidence in you.

Are there some decisions that leave you feeling confused and worried? They may be too big for you to decide on your own. Get help from an adult you trust. This will give you more confidence about future decisions.

Asset #27: Friendship-Making Skills

GOAL: To be good at making friends.

If you can't find friends in the usual places—school, your neighborhood, your place of worship—then look at your community as a whole. Is there a club or organization that matches one of your interests? Consider joining. You'll immediately have at least one thing in common with everyone else.

Start simply: Smile and say "hi." Ask people about themselves, and tell them something about you. Invite people to do things with you—go to a movie, study in the library after school, help you with a volunteer project.

Make an effort to form friendships with many different kinds of people. Diversity makes life more interesting. Valuing and appreciating diversity—which happens naturally when your friends are different ages, races, religions, ethnic backgrounds, and genders—is an essential step toward eliminating bias and prejudice.

Asset #28: Planning Skills

GOAL: To be good at planning ahead.

Some kids take life a day at a time. That's great—until they miss an important deadline, opportunity, or party.

If you're a poor planner, start simple: Make a daily to-do list. Number the items starting with "1" for most important. Check off items as you complete them. Move leftover items to the next day's to-do list. Once you get the hang of this, buy a planning calendar. Inexpensive ones are available at every office supplies store. Now you can start writing in future things to do— dates of long-term assignments, school holidays, upcoming social events.

If you're a terrific planner, put your skills to work and help to plan something big: a school carnival, a community event, the first-ever talent show in your congregation. Keep a journal of your experience. Afterward, summarize it on a single page, with emphasis on your responsibilities. This will look very good to a prospective employer or college admissions officer.

Asset #29: Self-Esteem

GOAL: To feel good about yourself.

Self-talk—the messages we give ourselves—can profoundly affect our self-esteem. When you make a mistake, what do you tell yourself? "It's no big deal; everybody makes mistakes"? Or "How could I be so stupid? I can't believe I did such a dumb thing." When you succeed at something, do you say to yourself, "Yes! I did it!" Or do you say, "I could have done better if I had really tried." In each example, the first statement is a self-esteem booster; the second is a self-esteem smasher.

Whenever you have a negative thought about your-self—when your self-talk makes you feel bad—then change it to a positive thought. Do this immediately. You'll feel better and you'll form the habit of self-affirmation, which most successful people share.

Asset #30: Hope

GOAL: To feel good about your future; to picture a happy future for yourself.

What do you see when you envision your future? Are you happy or sad? In a job you enjoy or bored out of your mind? Do you have healthy, loving relationships, or are you lonely?

Studies have shown that when people picture themselves reaching their goals, they improve their chances of this really happening. The dream comes true. That's one reason why it's important for you to picture a positive future for yourself. Even if you don't know how you will achieve the things you dream of, try to see them in your mind. Let your hope inspire you and guide you.

One way to create a positive future for yourself is to keep building your own assets. If you've been reading the "Tips for Teens" sections throughout this book, then you know which assets you already have and which ones you need to work on. The more assets you have, the better.

Roadblocks to Asset-Building and How to Overcome Them

For some kids, building assets can be relatively easy.

When kids come from strong families and strong communities—when they're surrounded by caring, loving people and systems of support—not much keeps them from building assets and benefiting from the positive opportunities they will encounter in life. But what about kids who don't fit this description? Some have been victimized by abuse. Others are growing up in poverty and may not have access to many positive activities and influences. Some are so bombarded with negative influences—stress, isolation, negative peer pressure, negative values—that the positive influences can't get through.

In our nationwide survey of 273,000 kids, we also identified and measured ten roadblocks to success for young people. We call these **developmental deficits.** The more deficits a child has, the less likely it is that he or she will build large numbers of assets. As a result, the child will be much more likely to make negative decisions and choices.

The deficits are:

1. Spending two or more hours a day alone at home without an adult

2. Putting a lot of emphasis on selfish values

3. Watching more than three hours of television a day

4. Going to parties where friends will be drinking alcohol

5. Feeling stress or pressure most or all of the time

6. Being physically abused by an adult

7. Being sexually abused

8. Having a parent who has a problem with alcohol or other drugs

9. Feeling socially isolated from people who provide care, support, and understanding

10. Having a lot of close friends who often get into trouble.

A lack of economic security can also undermine efforts to build assets. How do young people benefit from music lessons if they can't afford them? What good does it do to want to go to college if you can't pay for field trips in school? How can you be alert in school if you don't get enough to eat? How can parents build a strong, caring family if they have to work two jobs just to make ends meet?

These are serious, difficult questions that we must address as a society if we really want kids to succeed. So, while we concentrate on building assets, we must also make determined efforts to prevent deficits—to break down these roadblocks to health and well-being.

How to help kids overcome deficits.

Amid the bad news of deficits, there's also good news: Some young people beat the odds. Having deficits doesn't necessarily doom kids to failure. In spite of the barriers, some young people thrive. Why? Because they have important assets in their lives that balance out and even overcome the deficits.

There are five things that seem to make the most difference for young people with deficits:

▶ Getting them involved in structured, adult-led activities

▶ Setting boundaries and limits

▶ Nurturing a strong commitment to education

▶ Providing support and care in all areas of their lives, not just in the family

▶ Cultivating positive values and concern for others.

While it may not be as easy for these kids to build assets, they can do it. This doesn't always involve taking them out of a difficult situation, as much as we'd sometimes like to be able to do that. It doesn't always involve a lot of money. What seems to matter most is the presence of caring people who are cheering for them, giving them opportunities, and believing in them. Kids who have this kind of support can bounce back in amazing ways and live amazing lives.

Moving Toward an Asset Mindset

We know that assets can change kids' lives.

We know that when young people have enough of the developmental assets, both internal and external, they are much more likely to lead healthy, positive, productive lives. And they are much *less* likely to get involved in at-risk behaviors. Building assets in youth will free us as a society from spending our time and resources on crises and problems. But first, as a society, we must move toward an asset mindset.

There's an old African proverb: "It takes a whole village to raise a child." In other words, it's not enough for young people to hear a positive message at home *or* at school *or* in the community *or* at their place of worship. They need to hear the same message reinforced in all areas of their lives. That's why *What Kids Need to Succeed* includes ideas for parents *and* schools *and* communities *and* congregations–*and* teens themselves, because young people can build their own assets. Everyone has the potential to be an asset builder.

Here are six ways to get started.

▶ Read (or reread) "What Do Kids Really Need?" on pages 1–13 of this book. Look at the charts that illustrate the power of the assets to reduce at-risk behaviors and increase positive behaviors. Start telling other people about the importance of building assets for youth.

▶ Start reading newspaper stories about youth from a new perspective. When you read success stories about kids, try to identify which assets are present in their lives. When you read stories about kids with problems, think about which assets might be missing for them. How can you build those assets in your community?

▶ Invite a colleague, teacher, school counselor, social worker, religious leader, or youth worker you know to meet with you. Ask him or her to talk about his or her needs, interests, and concerns for your community. Introduce the concept of building assets in youth. Get his or her perspective. Bounce ideas around.

▶ Think about how you approach young people. Whether you work with youth in your own family, school, community group, or congregation, do you focus more energy on intervening in crises, preventing problems, or promoting assets? How can you shift more of your energy to asset-building?

▶ Share your thinking at a community meeting or event. Give people a chance to react and talk about the potential of what you have just described. Brainstorm ways your community can work together to build assets.

▶ Make a personal commitment to build one asset. Choose one that is important to you and make it a priority in your life. For example, you might become a mentor for a young person in your community. Or you may commit to spending more time at home with your children. Or you might undertake a family service project. Or you may decide just to be nicer to the kids in your neighborhood. No one alone can change a whole community, but everyone individually can make a significant difference.

What communities are learning about asset-building.

Your personal commitment is important. But it's also important that people begin thinking about how everyone *together* can build assets. How do we create neighborhoods, towns, cities, states, and even nations that put children first and make building assets a top priority? There's probably no single strategy that would work everywhere. But as communities have started asking that question, they've discovered some important principles that are shaping what they do.

Everyone has a role to play.

Not just parents, schools, community organizations, congregations, or governments, though they all certainly play important roles. *Everyone* can get involved in asset-building. Senior citizens and children, single adults and couples, policy makers and citizens, neighbors and employers, wealthy families and low-income families, liberals and conservatives—kids need us all. And we all can share a common, hopeful commitment to kids and the future.

Asset-building is more about people than programs.

Relationships are the key. Quality relationships can form with or without a program—a neighbor playing basketball with the kids, a grandmother keeping an eye on the bus stop to make sure that children are safe on their way to school. Programs may be vehicles for connecting youth to adults, but the critical issue is the care and support that grow through relationships. Money may help sometimes, but the commitment and involvement of caring people make the most difference.

Asset-building unleashes untapped resources.

Most people really do care about kids; they just don't know how to express that care in tangible ways. Most communities have great services for children and families, but they're all going in so many directions that they compete and conflict with one another. Asset-building gives people and organizations a clear, positive focus for their energy and resources.

All kids need asset-building.

Often youth programming focuses on just the "best" kids or the "worst" kids—the high achievers or the young people at risk. True, these groups may need special attention in some areas. But asset-building can help *all* kids. Communities are discovering the importance of designing strategies that can benefit a broad cross-section of youth, not just a targeted few.

Every community can improve.

Search Institute has studied hundreds of communities. While each community is different, no communities have very high levels of assets, regardless of region or size. Instead of trying to figure out who has more problems where, we all need to learn from each other.

Envisioning the asset-strong community.

As more communities everywhere start building assets, each community will remain unique in some ways, reflecting the personalities and priorities of the people who live there. But there are some things that likely will be in place in all asset-strong communities:

▶ Parents will have access to parent education and support that strengthens families and gives them skills in asset-building.

▶ Youth programs will make special efforts to ensure that all young people are involved in positive, constructive activities.

▶ Communities will develop a consensus on what's important to them—the positive values and norms they hope to pass on to the next generation.

▶ Teens will be seen as leaders and contributors in the community.

▶ Age segregation will be minimized so that kids regularly interact with people of all ages.

▶ Youth employers, teachers, and coaches will all have training in asset-building.

▶ School staff will pay as much attention to the school's climate as they do to the academic curriculum.

▶ Various organizations in the community that usually operate separately from one another—government, business, schools, families, congregations—will all cooperate on behalf of kids.

There are probably dozens more good things that will occur as communities become asset-strong. Most important, people in all parts of the community will have caught the vision, joined the asset-building team, and made a commitment to helping kids succeed. When that happens, the future will indeed be brighter—not just for kids, but for everyone.

Resources for Asset-Building

Almost any good book on parenting, teaching, or guiding kids contains information you can use to build assets in young people. As you become more involved in asset-building, you'll probably want to visit your local library or bookstore for additional resources. What follows are brief and selective lists of titles we recommend.

Resources for Parents

Bettner, Betty Lou, and Amy Lew, *Raising Kids Who Can: Using Family Meetings to Nurture Responsible, Cooperative, Caring and Happy Children* (New York: HarperCollins, 1992).

Clarke, Jean Illsley, *Self-Esteem: A Family Affair* (San Francisco: Harper San Francisco, 1985).

Edelman, Marian Wright, *The Measure of Our Success: A Letter to My Children and Yours* (New York: HarperCollins, 1993).

Elium, Don, and Jeanne Elium, *Raising a Son: Parents and the Making of a Healthy Man* (Hillsboro, OR: Beyond Words Publishing, 1992).

Elium, Jeanne, and Don Elium, *Raising a Daughter: Parents and the Awakening of a Healthy Woman* (Berkeley, CA: Celestial Arts, 1994).

Eyre, Linda, and Richard Eyre, *Teaching Your Children Values* (New York: Fireside, 1993).

Gordon, Dr. Thomas, *Discipline That Works: Promoting Self-Discipline in Children at Home and at School* (New York: NAL/Dutton, 1991).

Gordon, Dr. Thomas, *P.E.T.: Parent Effectiveness Training—The Tested New Way to Raise Responsible Children* (New York: NAL/Dutton, 1985).

Guarendi, Dr. Ray, and David Paul Eich, *Back to the Family: Proven Advice on Building a Stronger, Healthier, Happier Family* (New York: Simon & Schuster, 1991).

Leman, Dr. Kevin, *Bringing Up Kids without Tearing Them Down* (New York: Delacorte, 1993).

Louv, Richard, *Childhood's Future: Listening to the American Family—Hope and Solutions for the Next Generation* (New York: Doubleday, 1992).

Nelsen, Jane, and Lynn Lott, *Positive Discipline for Teenagers: Resolving Conflict with Your Teenage Son or Daughter* (Rocklin, CA: Prima Publishing, 1994).

Schulman, Michael, and Eva Mekler, *Bringing Up a Caring Child: Teaching Your Child to Be Kind, Just, and Responsible* (New York: Doubleday, 1994).

Steinberg, Laurence, and Ann Levine, *You and Your Adolescent: A Parent's Guide for Ages 10–20* (New York: HarperCollins, 1991).

Tracy, Louise Felton, M.S., *Grounded for Life?! Stop Blowing Your Fuse and Start Communicating with Your Teenager* (Seattle, WA: Parenting Press, 1993).

Whitham, Cynthia, M.S.W., *"The Answer Is No": Saying It and Sticking To It* (Pasadena, CA: Perspective Publishing, 1994).

Resources for Schools

Bloch, Douglas, *Positive Self-Talk for Children: Teaching Self-Esteem through Affirmations—A Guide for Parents, Teachers, and Counselors* (New York: Bantam, 1993).

Borba, Michele, and Craig Borba, *Self-Esteem: A Classroom Affair*, vols. 1 and 2 (San Francisco, CA: Harper San Francisco, 1984, 1985).

Curwin, Dr. Richard, *Rediscovering Hope: Our Greatest Teaching Strategy* (Bloomington, IN: National Educational Service, 1992).

Drew, Naomi, *Learning the Skills of Peacemaking: An Activity Guide for Elementary-Age Children on Communicating, Cooperating, Resolving Conflict* (Torrance, CA: Jalmar Press, 1987).

Jalongo, Mary Renck, *Creating Learning Communities: The Role of the Teacher in the 21st Century* (Bloomington, IN: National Educational Service, 1991).

Mendler, Dr. Allen, *What Do I Do When...? How to Achieve Discipline with Dignity in the Classroom* (Bloomington, IN: National Educational Service, 1992).

Nelsen, Jane, and H. Stephen Glenn, *Time Out: A Guide for Parents and Teachers Using Popular Discipline Methods to Empower and Encourage Children* (Fair Oaks, CA: Sunrise Press, 1992).

Noddings, Nel, *The Challenge to Care in Schools: An Alternative Approach to Education* (New York: Teacher's College Press, 1992).

Resources for Communities

Coles, Robert, *The Call of Service: A Witness to Idealism* (New York: Houghton Mifflin, 1993).

Gardner, John W., *Building Community* (Washington, D.C.: Independent Sector, 1991).

Hechinger, Fred M., *Fateful Choices: Healthy Youth for the 21st Century* (New York: Hill and Wang, 1993).

Leach, Penelope, *Children First: What Our Society Must Do—and Is Doing—for Our Children Today* (New York: Alfred A. Knopf, Inc., 1994).

Lofquist, William, *Discovering the Meaning of Prevention: A Practical Approach to Positive Change* (Tucson, AZ: Association for Youth Development, 1983).

A Matter of Time: Risk and Opportunity in the Non-School Hours (New York: Carnegie Council on Adolescent Development, 1992).

Reflection: The Key to Service Learning: A Guide for Program Leaders (New York: National Center for Service Learning in Early Adolescence, 1991).

Youth Service: A Guidebook for Developing and Operating Effective Programs (Washington, D.C.: Independent Sector, 1987).

Resources for Congregations

Christie, Les, *How to Recruit and Train Volunteer Youth Workers: Reaching More Kids with Less Stress* (Grand Rapids, MI: Zondervan, 1992).

Marcum, Walt, *Sharing Groups in Youth Ministry* (Nashville, TN: Abingdon Press, 1991).

Rydberg, Denny, *Building Community in Youth Groups* (Loveland, CO: Group Publishing, 1985).

Resources for Young People

Bernstein, Daryl, *Kids Can Succeed! 51 Tips for Real Life from One Kid to Another* (Holbrook, MA: Bob Adams, Inc., 1993).

Bingham, Mindy, Judy Edmondson, and Sandy Stryker, *Challenges: A Young Man's Journal for Self-Awareness and Personal Planning* (Santa Barbara, CA: Advocacy Press, 1984).

Bingham, Mindy, Judy Edmondson, and Sandy Stryker, *Choices: A Teen Woman's Journal for Self-Awareness and Personal Planning* (Santa Barbara, CA: Advocacy Press, 1984).

The Coping With... Series (New York: The Rosen Publishing Group, 1982–1993). Topics include feelings, health, friends, parents, self-esteem, school, the future, substance abuse, and more.

Eliot, Robert, and Dennis L. Breo, *Is It Worth Dying For? A Self-Assessment Program to Make Stress Work For You Not Against You* (New York: Bantam Books, 1989).

Kids' Random Acts of Kindness (Berkeley, CA: Conari Press, 1994).

Salzman, Marian, and Teresa Reisgies, *150 Ways Teens Can Make a Difference: A Handbook for Action* (Princeton, NJ: Peterson's Guides, 1991).

Schwartz, Linda, *What Do You Think? A Kid's Guide to Dealing with Daily Dilemmas* (Santa Barbara, CA: The Learning Works, 1993).

Schwartz, Linda, *What Would You Do? A Kid's Guide to Tricky and Sticky Situations* (Santa Barbara, CA: The Learning Works, 1991).

The Values Library (New York: The Rosen Publishing Group, 1990–1993). Topics include responsibility, compassion, honesty, citizenship, self-esteem, tolerance, morality, cooperation, and more.

Resources from Search Institute

Search Institute offers many practical resources for building assets in youth and creating healthy communities. Selected titles include:

▶ *Beyond Leaf Raking: Learning to Serve, Serving to Learn* by Peter L. Benson, Ph.D., and Eugene C. Roehlkepartain

▶ *Building Assets in Youth: The Power of Positive Youth Development,* a video featuring Peter L. Benson, Ph.D.

▶ *Healthy Communities, Healthy Youth* by Dale A. Blyth with Eugene C. Roehlkepartain

▶ *The Troubled Journey: A Portrait of 6th–12th Grade Youth* by Peter L. Benson, Ph.D.

▶ *240 Ideas for Building Assets in Youth,* a 22" x 30" color poster

▶ *Working Together for Youth: A Practical Guide for Individuals and Groups* by I. Shelby Andress.

To request a copy of our current catalog, write or call:

Search Institute
700 South Third Street, Suite 210
Minneapolis, MN 55415
Toll-free telephone: 1-800-888-7828
In Minneapolis/St. Paul: 376-8955.

Resources from Free Spirit Publishing

Founded in 1983, Free Spirit Publishing specializes in books and learning materials for kids, parents, and teachers. Many of our books address asset development. Selected titles include:

▶ *Bringing Up Parents: The Teenager's Handbook* by Alex J. Packer, Ph.D.

▶ *Directory of American Youth Organizations* by Judith B. Erickson

▶ *Fighting Invisible Tigers: A Stress Management Guide for Teens* by Earl Hipp

▶ *The Kid's Guide to Social Action: How to Solve the Social Problems You Choose—and Turn Creative Thinking into Positive Action* by Barbara A. Lewis

▶ *Making the Most of Today: Daily Readings for Young People on Self-Awareness, Creativity, and Self-Esteem* by Pamela Espeland and Rosemary Wallner

▶ *Respecting Our Differences: A Guide to Getting Along in a Changing World* by Lynn Duvall

▶ *Safe at School: Awareness and Action for Parents of Kids Grades K–12* by Carol Silverman Saunders

▶ *School Power: Strategies for Succeeding in School* by Jeanne Shay Schumm, Ph.D., and Marguerite Radencich, Ph.D.

▶ *Stick Up For Yourself: Every Kid's Guide to Personal Power and Positive Self-Esteem* by Gershen Kaufman, Ph.D., and Lev Raphael, Ph.D.

▶ *Talk with Teens about Self and Stress: 50 Guided Discussions for School and Counseling Groups* by Jean Sunde Peterson.

To request a copy of our current catalog, write or call:

Free Spirit Publishing Inc.
400 First Avenue North, Suite 616
Minneapolis, MN 55401-1730
Toll-free telephone: 1-800-735-7323
In Minneapolis/St. Paul: 338-2068.

Index

About the Authors

Peter L. Benson, Ph.D., has been president of Search Institute since 1985. He received his Ph.D. in social psychology from the University of Denver, his M.A. in psychology from Yale, and his B.A. in psychology from Augustana College. He is the author of several publications including *The Troubled Journey: A Portrait of 6th–12th Grade Youth* and *Growing Up Adopted: A Portrait of Adolescents and Their Families*, published by Search Institute, and *The Quicksilver Years: The Hopes and Fears of Early Adolescence*, published by Harper & Row.

Judy Galbraith, M.A., is the founder and president of Free Spirit Publishing Inc. in Minneapolis, creators of SELF-HELP FOR KIDS® books and learning materials. A former classroom teacher, she received an education degree from the University of Wisconsin at Steven's Point and holds a master's degree in guidance and counseling of the gifted from Norwich University in Vermont. She is the author of *The Gifted Kids Survival Guides* and coauthor of *Managing the Social and Emotional Needs of the Gifted* and *The Gifted Kids Survival Guide II,* all published by Free Spirit.

Pamela Espeland is the editor-in-chief for Free Spirit Publishing. She has authored or coauthored 13 books for children and adults including *Making the Most of Today: Daily Readings for Young People on Self-Awareness, Creativity, and Self-Esteem; Sexual Harassment and Teens: A Program for Positive Change;* and *Bringing Out the Best: A Resource Guide for Parents of Young Gifted Children,* published by Free Spirit. She has edited nearly 200 titles on a variety of subjects, specializing in nonfiction for young people, parents, and teachers. She graduated from Carleton College in Northfield, Minnesota.